THE BRIDGE BETWEEN

Nathan Vanek

Bluemoose

Copyright © Nathan Vanek 2006

First published in 2006 by
Bluemoose Books Ltd
25 Sackville Street
Hebden Bridge
West Yorkshire
HX7 7DJ

www.bluemoosebooks.com

British Library Cataloguing-in-Publication data

A catalogue record for this book is available from the British Library

ISBN 0-9553367-1-6

Printed and bound in Europe by the Alden Group

The Bridge Between is a compilation of articles first printed over a two-year period in The Low Down To Hull And Back News, the famous local Wakefield, Quebec, newspaper.

Acknowledgement
I would like to offer thanks to my friend and the owner of our
local newspaper, Nikki Mantell. I am happily in her debt for not
only initially inspiring the column, but for her generous support,
advice and constant encouragement.

Dedication
To Sharman, my true love, and to dad
You are that where the thought cannot reach. You are that high.
You are that Immortal Existence where no death can reach. You are
that Indivisible Whole which cannot be divided into soul, man,
woman or any kind of species. You are that which is Absolute,
Eternal, without any form and free from any sin. Human eyes
cannot see you. You are that.
Verse 263,
Light of Knowledge.
Swami Shyam.

1. Don't Sweat the Small Stuff

My parents live in what's called an adult building. That means no one under, I think, eighteen can live there. And when I'd travel from India over the years to see them, elderly residents would look at me as if I didn't belong at all. It was like the story of a slick New York professional walking into a tiny town in the Ozarks. The townsfolk, who all look like one another, watch as the fellow makes his way down the main street. The New Yorker feels more and more uncomfortable, aware of their unwelcoming stares. One grizzled old-timer picks up a stone and flings it. The old timer's cousin throws a rock. His cousin's wife, who's also his niece, tosses a bigger rock and the scene deteriorates quickly.

When I arrived in June, however, I was surprised and mortified to discover the old people in the building treated me as if I belonged there. I was not amused. For example, one morning on the elevator a fellow in yellow robe with matching slippers, hair all over the place, and face like a map of Vermont smiled a toothy smile up at me. "It's a very, very, very nice day today," he declared as if we met there regularly. I agreed completely though obviously neither of us had set even a toe outside up to that point of the morning. "Great to have only us old geezers here, aye?" I managed a smile of sorts that was probably more of a grimace. Then he honestly said, "Hey ho whaddya say we take a sauna together today?" I declined the invitation graciously. Then he asked, "What's the name again?" So I told the old fellow who I was, even though I knew full well he wouldn't recognise my name, probably because we'd never met in this life. As I got out at the ground floor I said, "Have a nice sauna." And he said, "What sauna?"

When I returned to the apartment I examined myself, again, in the mirror and, of course, I saw all the grey in my beard along with other unmistakable signs of growing old ... er.

When I first returned last summer, my uncle Ben and aunt Lucy decided to visit. They came via a taxi service for the elderly in Toronto called 'Wheel Trans.' My dad and I went down to meet their car in order to help them up to the apartment. As I lifted uncle Ben out of the taxi, he gave me a dollar tip. When he finally understood I wasn't the driver, he asked who the hell I was. After comprehending that I was his nephew, he asked for his dollar back, and he and I, dad and aunt Lucy began the slow shuffle to the elevators. Once we had finally arrived at the elevator doors, aunt Lucy realised she'd left her cane in the taxi. So I was sent quickly back to catch the car before it left, which was of course a most ridiculous notion. It had almost certainly finished its next run by then but I went anyway, walked outside for a few minutes and took my sweet time returning.

The conversation in the apartment revolved around the different types of canes available: white ones and brown ones, aluminium or natural wood, rubber tipped or not. My aunt described her visit to her doctor the previous week, which was the last time she'd gotten out of her house. The doctor had asked if she was in pain and she said only when she tried to do anything. He said she shouldn't be doing anything, and she responded by saying, "So who's doing? I'm not exactly a party animal." My uncle kept looking at me as though he couldn't understand why I was still there even after he'd tipped me. He certainly wasn't going to give me any more.

Their visit lasted less than an hour and a half, and I was rather sorry to see them leave. I enjoyed them. After the chatting and the tea, the biscuits and the drooling, we all sashayed slowly to the door, and dad and I trekked along with them down to their taxi. Aunt Lucy's cane was waiting for her even though it was a different car. I don't know how they did that. I opened uncle Ben's door for him and, just before he fell into the car, he took my hand in both of his, looked me straight in the eyes and said, "Nathan, over the years we've given you a hard time about the choices you've made. But, we can see you've found something good, and we just want you to know we have always loved you." Then my dad and I started back up to the apartment; he put his arm around me, and we decided we'd go for a sauna.

2. Phone Lines

For all but the last of the twenty-five years I spent in India, the idea of having a telephone never entered my mind. There would've been no point. It's not as if it would've worked. Near the end, however, and without any real upgrading of the infrastructure, little booths began popping up all over the country from which one could make local, national and even international calls.

Those booths invariably were tiny, airless cubicles with lights that could destroy your hair follicles in the time it took to call mommy. If, by chance, the attendant got through to your 'party' for you, which always felt rather like a miracle, a totally disjointed and horribly jumbled, confusing conversation would ensue. The connection would have an inherent echo and delay effect, resulting in both people talking at the same time, then both stopping and then both talking at the same time again. Also, you'd be cut off continually. A normal call might sound something like this;

"MOM? MOM? HOW ARE YOU? HOW'S MY PUPPY? HOW'S ... Oh for the love of God. Dial again will ya? MOM. MOM. WHAT? FIDO'S WHAT? FIDO'S WHAT? DEAD!!? IN BED? FED? WHAT DID YOU SAY?!! ... OH MARY MOTHER OF GOD! DIAL AGAIN!!"

After spending enough to feed a family of twelve villagers for a month in order to discover your dog is either dead or in bed, you'd fall out onto the street gasping for air with clumps of hair falling onto the pavement. Severely oxygen deprived, you knew that another few minutes might've meant brain damage. Staggering, trying to keep in mind it wasn't the lowly attendant's fault, you'd keep muttering your mantra 'God I hate this country. God I hate this country.' And God how I miss the place now.

Be that as it may, I wouldn't presume to criticise the phone system over here in western society since my return nor its effects on human life. The only aspect of this world that interests me, as I sit here today, is the cordless telephone, which was a brand new phenomenon to me.

Trekking through my family's cavernous condominium apartment in Toronto that first day back, I couldn't find the phone. I could hear it ringing, but I couldn't locate it. The thing seemed to be calling out from two or three places until I finally located it in my dad's den desk drawer. Then it took a while to figure out how to activate it. And so, of course, I said hello just in time to hear the caller hang up. I was unperturbed. I knew it wouldn't have been for me. It was most probably the Carps wanting to shuffle down the hall to play a few hands of Bridge with my parents.

As the days passed I became familiar with that new and amazing change in the telephoning experience. Having said that, however, I must add that old habits take time to change. I experienced an old dilemma, for example, while chatting with a long-ago girlfriend from Vancouver. She'd called just when I really should've been in the little boys' room, but I didn't want to interrupt the joy of re-uniting or re-connecting as it were. Meanwhile, as moments passed into several minutes, my small urge built into a driving necessity. I was in pain. Imagine my relief, then, as it dawned on me, like a message from above, that I could actually just get up and go. And so I certainly did.

It was positively a revelation. It was marvellous, although it did feel slightly strange doing that while talking to my lady-friend. And in the end it felt even stranger and really quite embarrassing when, after I mindlessly, automatically flushed the toilet, she said "Was that a toilet flushing!?"

3. You Can Bank On It

During the more than two decades I spent in India, the banking system progressed from trading cows and hiding currency under false floorboards to actual banks. During my last several years there, in fact, I placed what money I had in the Bank of Patiala.

One had to enter the bank by stepping over a chain, left, for some unknown reason, always across the front doorway. A very small man with a very large rifle sat just inside. The rifle was an ancient, double-barrelled affair slung proudly over his shoulder. A sign, hanging above the counter, read 'Please Count Yor Monys Befor Leving.' There were no computers and simple withdrawals or deposits could take the better part of a morning.

The day I was leaving for Canada, I asked to withdraw most of my funds, which amounted to some fifty thousand rupees, just under two thousand dollars Canadian. That may not sound like a king's ransom, but a normal withdrawal would consist of one or two less zeros made by a simple hill-person in town to purchase sugar for a special occasion or get a tooth pulled following a special occasion.

After some discussion amongst themselves, the teller came back to the counter. "That will not be possible sir. Very sorry," he said wagging his head from side to side smiling. Obviously, returning two days later was out of the question and so, after some further negotiations, we agreed I could indeed have my money, though in bundles of fives and tens. The fellow with the rifle was sent to the market for bags.

Back in Canada, I've since discovered banking has progressed without waiting for me. In my quest for respectability I've acquired all the right cards and made all the right moves. However, when I went to the office in Hull to pick up a license plate for my new really old car, I faced a huge dilemma. In order to finally grab the plate, sitting on the counter like the

Holy Grail itself, I had to pay $275.00, cash. I had handed the severe-looking lady my Visa card as I swelled with pride. But, she wouldn't accept it. I offered her a debit card. She refused. I didn't have a cheque or enough cash so she, with a show of tremendous forbearance, looking like wanting nothing more than to kick the family dog, suggested I go use the cash machine in the next building and come back. I had never used a cash machine. I knew I would eventually. I just wanted to wait for the right moment and that wasn't it. With people waiting at the license office and several looking over my shoulder at the cash machine, that was most certainly not the right time. There seemed to be a few slots, and I kept trying to stick the card in each of them. The lighting was poor and I was under no small pressure. I tried pushing the card into one or another aperture until I finally realised two of the slots were just lines. Of course I looked mentally challenged, and we all know what that means, as I tried to force my card into any mark that might've been the right place. I turned the card up and down and around, no doubt looking even more special, until the beast finally grabbed the thing.

With the card mercifully deposited in its proper receptacle, I next had to read the simple instructions. People came and went from the next machine while behind me the folks either giggled or groaned as they crowded in. My machine asked if I wanted FRENCH or english. The arrow seemed to point between the buttons. I thought I pressed for english, but got FRENCH, had to start again. More giggles. More groans. I knew my secret code, but made a couple more mistakes before figuring the whole thing out. I punched in my desired amount, $275.00 including the decimal point, waited, waited, got my card back, waited and then got rejected. No one likes rejection. I tried everything again and I was rejected again. A voice from the now raucous crowd behind called out in a sarcastic tone, "It's gotta be in multitudes of twenty." I thanked the man without turning around, consoled by the thought that I'd probably never see any of them again, finally got the money and positively slithered out. As I re-entered the licence office, people were looking downright nasty. The lady behind the counter had her head in her hands and I felt sorry for her puppy. I paid my money, grabbed the plates and drove off into a new world.

4. The Art of Flying

The NEWS' meditation expert says; Nothing to fear from Yogic flyers.
January 28, 1999

It's not surprising to hear that the beauty of Chelsea has attracted the Transcendental Meditation™ Group. And Jean-Claude Pommet, the person who wants to build a subdivision in Chelsea based on 'Natural Law,' obviously has known the area well. He seems to bring into his project, to build one-hundred-and-fifty new homes all facing in a particular direction, an appreciation for the district. He also obviously brings along a love for the teachings of the Maharishi Mahesh Yogi.

Whether or not his plans are economically and practically good for the area and whether having a Maharishi Arya-Vedic college there would be nice for the people of the area, as well as safe and wholesome, are two very different questions. I'm not qualified to answer the first, but I certainly can shed some light on the second.

Pommet is quite correct in his assertion that meditation is a scientific technique that can prevent and solve problems, social or personal. However, when he includes so-called Yogic flying in his statement and in their teachings, meditation is undermined. In fact, in my opinion, the ancient and proud technique of meditation is made to look downright silly. There's nothing scientific about encouraging grown men and women to leap around like frogs or believe they should learn to levitate unless it's the science of how to leapfrog people out of their savings. The Maharishi comes from an ancient and proud tradition of yogis. But, again in my opinion, I'm afraid that he has been long influenced and compromised by the ambitious, greedy business people around him.

Sanskrit mantras, the phrases given for students to repeat during meditation, are all essentially having the same meaning. They all mean that we're one life, that the source of every form, seen or unseen, black, white,

Christian, Jew, Hindu, Buddhist, big or small, is one and the same. The practice can have a very deep and powerful influence on our lives. There's no reason to be secretive about these mantras, as the TM teachers are trained to be. Meditation, simple and un-mystical, is a key to unlock the mysteries of this existence. It was discovered by sages, handed down from generation to generation and should be treasured, protected, employed with gratitude and a pure heart.

Several years ago Alan Abel, then writing for the Toronto Globe and Mail and now with the National Post, visited the Himalayas to interview Swami Shyam, mostly because Brian Mulroney's sister lived at the school. She wouldn't speak to him so Alan had to settle for the Swami. Since I was also there at the time, I remember the great answer Swami Shyam gave to the question about whether he had mystical powers. "Yes I do," he said, "I have the power to love everyone unconditionally".

Having said all that, I should add I'm certain the people who want to build the TM homes and the Arya-Vedic college in Chelsea are good people. There's nothing to fear. They can build their houses facing any direction they think will bring them peace of mind. We can all try Reiki, crystal healing, Tibetan singing bowls, Feng Shui, astrology. It's all nice and may even help us. I've seen ascetics buried up to their necks for months at a time. I've seen men with withered arms from having held them aloft for years at a time. I've seen men and women who could tell my past in detail, snake charmers, yogis walking on hot coals, Brahma bulls who could answer questions. But, really, sooner or later every thinking person will have to get back to the basics if he's serious about being free of fear, bigotry, ignorance. The rest may be harmless, as Mr Pommet's plans certainly are, but it's all frills.

5. Snow Cloud Heaven

During a nasty blizzard one night a couple of weeks ago, I stopped to help a lady. Her car was sitting derelict at the side of Highway 105. As I stepped out of my trusty little Toyota, the lady ran up and asked if I could jump her. That just never happened in all the twenty-three years I spent in India. Anyway, I whipped out my cable, gave her a jolly good boost and got her going. I love the way people here help each other through the winter travails. Stories about the '98 Ice Storm are told, perhaps ad nauseum, of kindness and neighbourliness.

When first I saw Wakefield and this whole area, the summer gods and goddesses of fertility had conspired to show off the hills at their best. The fields were green, pollen drifted in the air and as my friend Lori, who I'd come to visit, and I drove along the River Road, I kept muttering that I was having a cosmic experience. It just seemed that the river was talking to me. And as a bonafide tree-hugger and granola-crunching mystic type from a mystical land, if anyone could talk to nature it should be me.

Then came winter and I couldn't hear a damned thing. Winter was not a cosmic experience and, in fact, I felt a fear fermenting in my tummy. Of course it may have been something I ate. I had a vague, distant memory of shovelling a little snow from a lane in Toronto with my plastic, red shovel. But I never thought I might have to shovel several feet of the stuff repeatedly before breakfast. It certainly never occurred to me I'd ever live some place where I'd have to shovel snow from my roof, that I'd have to go trudging waist deep to the side of my house with an extension pole.

In India, by and large, the problem is heat. Middays during the hot season in central India people lie low, so low in fact they're often underground trying to stay cool. I've been to the state of Bihar in June when livestock and even people often succumb to the heat. I was once sitting on a curb in Bodh Gaya sipping a coke when a bird fell right out of a tree and landed with a pathetic little thud beside me. An emaciated old man with blood-shot eyes came along wearing only a loincloth and sat down next to me. Granted, he wouldn't have passed dress-code at the Hyatt-Regency Hotel, but I nevertheless thought it rude of him to keep glaring at me and my coke, at me and my coke, again and again. His tongue was hanging from the corner of his mouth, drooling. Unfortunately, I'd just gulped down the last of the drink and, anyway, it wasn't such a cold one and the sugar would have been bad for his teeth.

So you see, after the first shock I began to almost even maybe enjoy winter here. Danny patiently, good naturedly came each time I called to check every odd little sound I noticed my furnace making and I began to see the beauty of this snow-cloud heaven of Wakefield winter. And now, anything above minus 15 is fine with me. I've skated in Rupert, gone tobogganing with Jake behind the Wakefield community centre, seen the hockey at the arena in Low. But, it's still the people here who give me a jolly good boost and really get me going.

6. Animal Crackers

On my way to Canada, I spent a couple of weeks in London, England. My friends there had an old skinny, black cat suffering stoically from feline cancer. They'd taken Bella, which was her name, to the free RSPCA veterinarian clinic weekly for some time and I tagged along on their last visit.

There were no pure-breeds at the RSPCA. They jumped all over each other barking, snorting, crying, whining, clawing, howling. They slid along the linoleum floor, scratched the walls, and so did their pets. But everyone was friendly. Everyone cared. Since Bella hadn't been improving, however, my friends decided to take her to a clinic uptown, the type that accepts appointments and Visa cards; it wasn't quite the way I had envisioned seeing London.

That waiting room had nice carpeting and papered walls with paintings of graceful animals running through fields. It smelled good. Brochures piled neatly on the receptionist's marble desk explained proper grooming techniques. A Collie and a Dalmatian sat obediently beside their owners. A Siamese cat lay complacently in its portable cage. I could've lived there. After a careful examination and medicine, which included pills and an injection, the doctor declared confidently that, as long as Bella was brought each week for further treatment, she 'could look forward to several more months of good quality life.' The doctor was so confident I wondered if I shouldn't ask for an injection myself.

By the middle of that same night we knew he'd been horribly wrong. And there was to be no question about quality of life. As Bella was breathing her last (and making quite a mess on the carpet) my friends, in a panic, phoned an emergency service for family pets. I rather thought they'd have been better advised to phone an emergency cleaning service, but they soon saw it was too late in any case. The phone was handed to me and I told the drowsy doctor the sad news and he said, "Give my condolences to the family".

India's a little different. Suffice it to say it's often not quite so genteel. Although dogs are sometimes pets, though never cats, most are strays. Pure-breeds are getting popular now, but I doubt you'll see doggie pooper-scoopers any time soon. Doggie breath fresheners, of course, are out of the question. And in the mountains, where I lived, the animal support system was a tad weak.

However, there was one stray dog that became a favourite in the area. One day Ralph, which was his name, went all peculiar. He was found in convulsions at the side of the road choking, shaking and thrashing about with wobbly back legs. Of course, the same thing happens to me on my bad days, but I usually don't try biting off my own genitals. Mercifully, I can't reach. At just that same time, I had been doing something rather doggie-like with a lovely lady other than my girlfriend. And my girlfriend came banging at my door yelling, hollering, "Ralph is choking, Ralph is choking!" Within a moment I was running down the hillside behind her, freaked out, trying to straighten my trousers, having left a lady cowering under my bed.

A large crowd had gathered round Ralph. They were watching, trying to decide what to do. People were calling out, "Do something for God's sake!" "What to do? What to do?" "Help Ralphie," "Mad dog! Stone him!" Things like that. In the midst of all the uproar I ran through the crowd, grabbed the cadaverous-looking canine from behind, picked him up and began doing the Heimlich manoeuvre on him. It was quite a sight. I was basically showing everyone what I had just been doing up in my cabin. Nothing dramatic happened. There was no projectile vomiting, nothing came out. But, believe it or not Ralph was much better after that, I was hailed as a hero and that dog became strangely attached to me afterwards.

So as I walk the street and alley of Wakefield now, I watch my neighbours with their pets. I appreciate the way Hugh relates to his noble husky, the way Hannah talks to her golden labrador or Michael cares for that big old black labrador who's always trying to get into the Chez Eric at lunch time. But, I'm especially fond of that funny-looking, clever black mutt that hangs around the Radisson Expeditions building. He or she reminds me somehow that there's a bit of India here with me still.

7. There's No Insurance

Upon returning from my little trip to India, a trip that lasted twenty-five years, I hunkered down with my seventy-nine and eighty-three-year-old parents in Toronto. I'm sorry, but that's where I'm from. On the third evening, while waiting for mom to boil up the broccoli, I sidled up to the cookie jar and lifted the lid. As I reached in, mom slapped my hand. "Not before dinner!" she barked. After realising I wasn't having my first stroke, I managed to squeak, "Mom, I'm forty-seven." "Doesn't matter to me, buster," was her classic response. So I moved to Wakefield.

Of course it wasn't that simple. Once here I needed a car. Everyone's got a car here, usually a four-wheel-drive with a husky sitting in the passenger seat. Buying a car's easy, but try getting someone to insure you after so many years away. Since I purchased the thing in Hawksbury, which is a story in itself, I tried to insure it there, in Ontario.

The licence office wouldn't give me the plates without the insurance. And the insurance companies wouldn't give me the time of day. One company agreed to insure me, for about twice what I paid for the car. Needless to say there was no sense in pointing out that I'd been driving in conditions that make the roads of Canada look like a kiddie's ride at the fairgrounds. (Let's ignore that curve at Pine Road for the moment). The florid-faced agent behind the desk, the one I was trying to curry favour with and shook hands with as though I wanted his baby, would not understand. He'd likely have his first real religious experience were he to drive just for ten minutes down the Delhi-Jaipur Trunk road. He'd have to figure out how to drive along with bullock carts, tractors, out-of-control interstate buses, camels, trucks passing on the wrong side, cows wandering wherever they pleased. He'd come across herds of water buffalo, as he careened around corners, looking like potentially prehistoric road-kill. And he'd encounter all of it obviously at speeds that varied widely and at any moment.

Needless to say, the problem was that I had no record of insurance, no driving record, no life in fact. Essentially, they told me to get a life and then come back. And I thought I'd have a life if I had a car. Or I thought, at least, I could get a life if I had a car and maybe eventually even a husky. I drove the car on a ten-day permit, insured on the vendor's policy, which made the vendor more than a little nervous, up to Wakefield. Not knowing that Quebec's a different country, I assumed I still had a problem. It was a beaten and hopeless shadow of a man who walked, hunched over, in through the door of the Mallette/McLennan Assurances building that day.

They welcomed me. I was even invited to sit in a chair, make my request, say my piece and then Stephen smiled and said, "Oh, ok. I can do that for you." And he did that for me, at a fraction of the price it'd be in Ontario even under normal circumstances. Then he explained the system in Quebec, what to do and what to watch out for. He marched me through the procedure step by step. It was better than a chiropractor.

So it was time to get a life. The biggest hurdle in my quest for a license plate, I'd been warned, was still the safety check. I had my little car looked over again by a certified mechanic, which I could tell he was by the black under his fingernails. Then I found the safety check place in Hull, walked into the office and handed over the keys. I was nervous, a condition exacerbated by a fellow sitting in the waiting area who kept grinning like he knew something private about me that no one should know. He flipped through magazines scarcely without looking at them, smiling up at me again and again until he blurted out, "I bin ere four time four car never first time pass up to dis day." I swore to him that MY car was going to make it. We sat in that room like expectant fathers, waiting to hear that our kids came out with all their faculties in order.

Well, he was right and I was wrong. I had to go fix something ridiculously small. As I left, we grinned at each other in a mutually defeated sort of way, and at least I knew he and I had bonded. I fixed what needed fixing within an hour and then again I sat in that office flipping through magazines. As I waited, a young guy came in and nervously handed over his keys. I couldn't help myself. I kept grinning up at him.

8. The Gandhi Dental Clinics

When first I returned from what I call my little trip to India, I visited a friend living the good life in Los Angeles. Something was different about him. He looked somehow better and it wasn't until I was well into my veggie-burger at dinner that I realised what it was. He had the whitest and most perfect set of teeth I'd ever seen. It occurred to me that those tusks could fetch a pretty penny on the open market today and that he'd better watch out for poachers. Predictably, just as I entertained those thoughts I broke one of the crowns covering my uneven teeth. My buddy suggested he lead me to his dentist straight away, but I didn't have a diaper with me. My lower inner organs dissolve at the mere thought of having to visit a dentist. They scare the bejesus out of me, and I never trust anyone who doesn't feel somewhat the same. It'd be like trusting someone who doesn't like dogs, like most of my relations for example.

Fresh in my memory is the last time I had to visit a dentist, in New Delhi, just before leaving for the real world. I had a rather intrusive little procedure done that left me lying in my hotel room that night wondering if there really is a God. My dentist phoned to ask how I was and I said, "How d'ya think I am, you bathtard! You told me it'd be thimple (spit, splutter, drool). I'm lying here in pain, drugged up to my eyeballs, incontinent, throbbing and the TV's broken! Where were you during the thecond world war you nazi?!"

Actually, what I said was, "I'm ok, doctor. How are you?" He said he was fine and suggested I 'talk' to my teeth and send them good vibrations. It's one of the peculiarities of being known as some sort of mystic type that folks from all walks of life tend to give me teachings, even dentists. (My friend in L. A., a comedy writer, says people are always trying jokes out on him.) So I quickly and with what I thought was tremendous wit responded, "I talk to them all the time, doc (spit, sputter, drool). I tell them to fuck off regularly." Unfortunately, that comment precipitated a scolding for my bad attitude, and a rather lengthy dissertation on the power of the mind. In retrospect, since getting my life somewhat back together, I can see he meant well. But, at the time all I could think was how my life's come down to being lectured on the power of the mind from 'a … a … dentist'.

Now, you may think that I should've just waited 'til I got to Canada before doing that dental work, and you'd have a point, though you must either be a plumber or on a dental plan. I've been to some very good dentists in India. They're all dead now, but one or two have spawned offspring.

Dentistry in India's a three-tier affair; believe me when I tell you that, in the nearly two and a half decades I spent there I had the full range of experience. For the simple folk who sleep with the family cow and who put salt in their lentil soup only on special occasions, there's a type of dental shop one sees on the side of any road, at Spring fairs, or at religious gatherings. And if you weren't religious before visiting that dentist, you would be afterwards. A man, usually wearing a turban, sits in full lotus position on a blanket with a wooden sign beside him. The sign would read 'Gandhi Dental Clinic' above a badly painted smiling mouth with grotesquely large, white teeth. In front of the dentist, and I use the term loosely, a variety of medieval-looking instruments would be arranged next to a display of plastic dentures. It would cost 25 rupees to have a tooth yanked, the equivalent of about 70 cents.

Next, for the hill-people equivalent of a middle-class, there existed a type of dentist like the one I was somewhat familiar with in the town where I lived. In fact, there was a time when it seemed I should just rent a room at his clinic. The name of the place was 'The Gandhi Dental Clinic.' To access it one had to walk through a maize of ramshackle stalls for fixing shoes, selling fruits and cutting hair. One had to brave a set of rickety wooden steps to the second floor and slip through a curtained doorway into a cramped waiting room. A large desk, with a set of snapping plastic teeth as paperweight and a penholder with no pens, filled most of the waiting room, leaving a little area for two wooden benches. People of all sorts would crowd onto those benches holding each other's heads, rocking back and forth while others stared wide-eyed at scary posters showing varied and horrific dental or gum problems.

Before entering the actual clinic, one had to remove one's shoes. The dentist tried his darndest to be hygienic, which is not a concept that comes easily up there. He was slow, meticulous, and really didn't like making mistakes. Of course, it was disconcerting when the electricity would go off again and again in the middle of a drilling or a root-canal procedure; but the overhead fan kept some of the flies away and disposable syringes were actually used.

The alternative to the previously described clinics was to travel 12 or 14 hours to New Delhi by road or give up your first born in order to afford the plane-fare to visit the beautiful, modern, even swanky 'Gandhi Medical Clinic.' Matchless in elegance and so well outfitted that I could've happily lived in the foyer, it boasted an impressive list of clients. As a matter of fact, the dentist there had a nasty habit of pulling out his autograph book when you had a mouth full of cotton and silver-handled instruments. The proud, portly doctor would shove the pages up to your swollen face to point out the names of Indira Gandhi, Rajiv Gandhi, Maneka Gandhi and every other Gandhi available, as one did one's best to make gurgling sounds of appreciation. You don't want to alienate the fellow at a time like that. But, he was and is a good dentist and often checked up on you after particularly intense sessions, even offering free teachings on the healing power of the mind.

Which pretty much brings us full circle. And I hope my readers understand that I've offered this description of dentistry in India at considerable risk to myself since there's always a danger in writing or talking about dentistry as if your troubles are all behind you. It's a kind of jinx. Something unfortunate tends to happen soon after. In fact, I wanted to describe dentistry in India only after visiting the clinic here in Wakefield, but I think hell will freeze over first. Although I've heard many good things about the place, that they're gentle, thorough and reasonable, my message to them there is simple: don't hold your breath.

9. Snapping Turtles

One of the pieces of information I've come across since returning after so many years in India, which really shocked and amazed me, concerns the penis size of snapping turtles. It's not a bit of trivia, and I even hesitate to use the term, that I'd likely be subjected to in India. Over there, you're more likely to see headlines like, 'Idols of Lord Ganesh Shock Devotees-Drinks Milk!" It seems that the reproductive organs of the Lake Ontario Snapping Turtles are fifteen percent shorter than what they ought to be. That must really get them snapping. And it's just no good using the age-old excuse about being in the bath too long. They ain't getting any bigger.

Apparently, some University of Guelph zoologists spent years studying the shrivelling penises of the turtles. And while one has to wonder what the zoologist's own home life must be like, what motivates them to delve into such research, what drives them on, in fact, one has to applaud their diligence, not to speak of their passion for detail. Turtle eggs that were collected also produced turtles with other deformities or never hatched at all, a far preferable alternative from my point of view. This problem, allegedly, is due to the PCBs, dioxins and furans, otherwise known as gender-bender chemicals.

According to the same article, on March 7th in the Ottawa Citizen, the salmon in Lake Erie are also losing their male traits, the heavy jaw and red, cherubic colour, for the same or similar reasons. Which makes me think about inviting a few of the guys I've met around here down to my cousin's cottage on Lake Erie for an afternoon swim. The article also points out that young Florida alligators, subjected to a pesticide spill, had very small penises and abnormal testicles. And Herring Gulls on the Great Lakes are being called now by the dubious handle of Gay Gulls.

The point of all this, and why I remain even days later struggling with temptation to prove that I'm alright in various strange and unseemly ways, is that recent findings show men in Europe and North America mirror these findings in wildlife. And while the women of the species, if now given the chance to take over, may finally get it right, it bothers me. And I haven't even brought up yet the case of the Mudpuppies in the St. Lawrence, the Ottawa River and the Great Lakes. They're turning up with extra, missing or fused toes, and missing or misshapen legs. I've always said, dear God fuse my toes, bend a leg, but don't do to me what you're doing, in your inexplicable wisdom, to those poor snapping turtles.

At a certain point it just is no good to say size doesn't matter or that it's all in how you use the thing. Call me sentimental, but I also don't like to hear any creature with a name like Mudpuppy having such problems. It'd be better to use their former nicknames, quoted in the same article, of water devil, thing, monster and moron, names I've often called my male organ, actually.

Around eighteen years ago, on my first ever visit to Ottawa, I was helping a friend paint his front room when I read a news article, on the paper under my feet, concerning acid rain. According to that article, which scared the stuffing out of me at the time, acid rain was going to end life as we know it within five years. Whatever may be the case, whatever may be the future of life as we know it, a little enlightenment certainly would come in handy when subjected to doomsday information like that. It behoves us to know something of where we've come from and where we're going while doing the best we can for our families and this mixed up world. I won't say it's my experience, but I've read in books, thereby making it all the more believable, that held deep within the heart-space of every living being is an eternal spark of life. And that the source from where you're reading these few words and from where I write them is one and the same source of that life. It works for me.

In any event, and no matter what our respective experiences, philosophies or beliefs may be, I'd like to suggest a few moments of silence for the Florida alligators, the gay gulls, the Mudpuppies, and especially for our poor unfortunate snapping turtles.

10. Milk Builds Strong Bodies

According to popular belief, even before the Indo-Aryans made their way from the Russian Steppes down through Iran and the Hindu Kush into what is known today as India, their lives were centred around the cow. She was the symbol of a mother's unconditional love. She was their measure of wealth. The cow gave them milk, butter, cheese and dung for fuel; they probably shared many intimate moments together. The cow was an object of fierce attachment. Which was one of the reasons the Aryans got so ticked off when the local folk, who had never seen a cow before, kept pilfering them. Still, and as everyone knows, the cow is worshipped in India.

Years ago, while at a Vipassana monastery in the south, I had gone to a tailor for a new courte. That's a light, cotton type of shirt. The tailor was sitting with his machine and what must have been the whole of his extended family on their front porch. While I waited for some buttons to be sewn more or less into place, the sky turned from clear and blue to cloudy and dark. Then the sky turned from cloudy and dark to downright malicious. Within twenty minutes the monsoon season began with a vengeance. The rain and wind were so strong it was all I could do to hang on to the balcony post. The tailor had his legs around the post and his arms around his machine. That left the rest of the family to fend for them selves. I suppose it was a matter of priorities. The new courte flew up over the rooftops and we all watched a big old cow, black and white and wet all over, being swept down the street on its side. It was bellowing helplessly as the whipping rain and the force of the wind took total control.

The storm subsided as quickly as it had begun. The sky remained ominous, but the wind and the rain mercifully subsided. The tailor busied himself with re-organising his corner and his family before beginning a new courte. That's one of the remarkable qualities of the Indian people in general. They just truck on with a minimum of fuss or bother. So I sat and waited, soaked to the skin but warm enough. And as the courte began to take shape we were all amused to see that same cow sauntering back just as leisurely as if it were a daily ritual. People were going out onto the street and touching its feet or tail for good luck, myself included.

Up in the mountains where I lived there's no D and D Dairy, no Pritchard's Dairy Farm. There's no Depanneur Proprio with its variety and sizes of milk cartons. You'll not find a choice of 2% partly skimmed, skimmed, homogenised, or half-and-half milk, not to speak of chocolate, clotted cream, sour cream or the ever popular whipped cream. Up there, milk's just milk, still delivered to your door by one of the two hulking figures known throughout the area as the cow ladies. They make their rounds each day pouring the precious stuff into the can you leave hanging on a nail.

Many people in the area think our cow ladies may actually date back to the days of the first Indo-Aryan invasions. They're ancient. One is mostly blind, while the other can hardly walk. Their husband is totally deaf, which is just as well since the way they talk to their cows is a bit of a turn-off. The cow ladies spend most of their time grunting endearments to the grazing beasts. 'Unh unh. Mmmoo. Unh unh. Mooo.' After centuries of that, one can only imagine what the bedroom chatter must be like. They have a near total monopoly on the milk trade in the area, the only other company being a one-cow operation run by a homosexual farm boy affectionately known as the dairy queen. When he was a little younger he delivered his milk with a real flair, usually dressed in a long flowing velvet gown, pink scarf blowing in the wind. And I personally felt a little sorry when he began toning it down.

Not long before I left India, there was a major argument between the cow ladies and one of their customers, who complained that the milk had been watered down. "You very lying cheating people," the man yelled. "You putting water inside milk putting isn't it!" A crowd had gathered as usual and accusations were flung from side to side. Thankfully, however, that's all that got flung. It really came down to whether we were willing to believe the cow ladies or not. They insisted the problem was that their cows were drinking too much water. As scientifically unlikely as that was, I was willing to take them at their word, largely because I didn't care.

There was one occasion on which I did get quite put off with them. There's nothing quite like going to fetch one's milk, start up the old cookstove for the morning tea and toast, only to find that instead of cow milk there's cow urine in the can. Tends to put you off your rhythm. One of my neighbours, it turned out, was involved in an old Aryuvedic healing technique, which required a spoonful of cow urine to be mixed with certain herbs. I don't know whether it was for cancer, beriberi or hair loss, and it really didn't matter to me. There is, then, something to be said for cartons of milk, like the fact that one can be fairly sure that milk will be found in them. But, I do tend to miss the rather more organic, even earthy style still found up there in those middle ranges of the Himalayan mountains and the musical morning sounds of clanking tin cans.

11. Ships In The Night

When satellite television first crept onto the Indian entertainment scene, with many western channels, one of my friends declared he wouldn't get a television because he'd just watch it all the time. I felt compelled to point out that probably that's why the manufacturers supply on and off switches. But, now that I have a computer I'm not at all sure my sarcasm was really appropriate.

For most of my years in India, the most sophisticated piece of technology I owned was an old short-wave radio. Now that I live in Canada, my computer's opened up a whole new world to me. My eyes are finally open. I've looked into every site from local news to adult web pages. I was in a particularly raunchy sort of chat room, late one night, when a lady 'whispered' to me. That's a mechanism whereby you can carry on a private chat with someone. She wrote, 'Hey, Tercel, if you wanna do me, click here. Click hard!'

I couldn't find her name on the room list but I clicked anyway. And I clicked hard. In fact, I clicked so hard I feared for the life of my computer. After two decades in a place where bare ankles or shoulders are considered scandalous, you'd better believe I clicked hard. I never returned to any chat room like this one, however, after I saw the way my email inbox looked the next evening. The list, which shows who sent messages to me that day, read something like this; mom and dad, Peter, Francis, Aunt Phyllis, TEEN SLUTS, mom and dad. NAKED CELEBRITIES, George and Amy, HORNY COUPLES, mom and dad . . .

Anyway, after wandering from room to room lately, I ended up in website called Bisexual Coffee House. For a while I sat back and watched what conversations were going on until one caught my fancy. It was between a fellow called Fishfry and a girl called Saucylady. Saucylady kept insisting that she'd never fall in love because she's been 'demolished.' I felt

Fishfry was not really being very sensitive or even particularly nice. Saucylady said she'd still have sex, but never love. Sounded like good, sound logic to me, and that's when I felt impelled to jump into the conversation.

"What kind of name's Fishfry anyway?" I asked. "Each to his own," he answered deftly. 'Did you have fish for dinner?" I badgered. Then I saw, "Bye, Saucylady. I'm tired and Tercel's badgering me." Then, as always when someone logs off, I saw 'Fishfry has left the conversation.' Saucylady wrote "You badgered him, Tercel." And I said "No I didn't. He must've had bigger fish to fry." Saucylady typed "Ha Ha. You're funny." And then I whispered to her "What happened, Saucyone. What demolished you?"

What ensued was a two-hour conversation that held within it some of the loveliest and most powerful moments I've ever shared with a lady in my adult life. Of course, we all know what that says about my adult life, but suffice it to say we laughed, she cried 'cause real men don't cry, and eventually it came time for me to describe myself. She had already described herself. I'm not sure if it was the forty-eight year old part or the twenty-three years in India part, but next thing I knew, I was seeing 'Saucylady has left the conversation.' I was stunned. I was, in fact, demolished. I stared at the screen for a half-hour until I decided I'd never fall in love again. I'd still have sex, but not love.

At the same time next evening, I went straight to the same chat-room. I looked on the list of names there, but saw no sign of Saucylady. In any event, I typed in, "Has anyone seen my Saucylady?" A few minutes later I typed it in again and, to my surprise, I received a whisper from a lady calling herself Playtex. "I hope you find your lady, Tercel." I thanked her and then asked; "Why did you choose that name?" to which she responded simply, "I like it." So I came back with the snappy remark "It's a stretch, but works for me."

A few Moments later Playtex whispered to me, "Tercel, can I ask you a question?" "Please do," I wrote. "What should I do if I've fallen in love with someone on the Internet?" I thought before answering. "I guess you should ask him what he's feeling. What have you got to lose?" Playtex wrote, "ok". And then I saw 'Playtex has left the conversation.'

12. Rats

One early morning, as the sun just began to shyly peek from behind clouds, I sat on my carpet feeling the warmth. I was meditating. I was one with the universe. I was not just an individual human, but the whole ocean of life itself when I felt a strange tingling in my toes. The tingling spread upwards onto my legs and I was convinced it was the beginning of a true religious experience, the opening of the famous serpent power kundalini. I was infused with a profound and pervasive sense of bliss, until I realised it was in fact a mouse running around my legs.

Upon opening my eyes we stared at each other, that little mouse and I, until he or she scurried away with its tail between its legs. And although I'd have preferred a transcendental experience, there was something reassuring about coming face to face with the fellow. I hadn't seen any rodent since leaving India where it's pretty hard to not be faced with them, one way or another. I'll not describe the pneumonic plague epidemic in Gujarat or the mouse I found dead in my honey jar one morning. I won't even begin to describe what it felt like to find a mouse in my pants as I put them on, which made two mice in my pants, or when a big one landed on my head as it fell from a broken wall behind where I was sitting. Suffice it to say they're just always in your face, a part of life; and now I see they're following me to the New World.

On my way out of India, for example, I visited a dermatologist in New Delhi who prescribed a certain cream to help ward off the effects of the Indian sun on my boyish good looks. I began slathering the stuff all over my face twice each day until long after I had left the motherland. One morning, however, as I spread it around, I began to read where, in tiny little words on the tube, was written, 'This medicine has proved to be carcinogenic in rats and mice.' You may think me alarmist, but that bothered me. It just kept gnawing away at me. I found it difficult to spread the stuff on. My hand slowed, stopped altogether and then I sat down in a chair to think the matter over.

While not professing to be an intellectual giant, I don't think even the simple-minded among us would have trouble figuring out what was wrong with that picture. So, with cream half covering my face, I picked up the phone and dialled India. When I was finally able to talk to the doctor I told him of my fears and that even though I've been called a rat upon occasion, and even though some of my best friends are rats, it just seemed somehow wrong. He reassured me, however, that all was well and I should just go ahead and use the stuff. And I did, for a few more days. But every time I put on the cream I felt I was putting on cancer.

You may have noticed an article in the Ottawa Citizen on March 12th about how rats have helped four sterile Italian men father children. And without getting into details I would point out that many folks there have denounced the practice, stating that it could have 'unpredictable genetic consequences.' I tend to agree; and if I was one of those Italian stallions, I'd keep a close eye on my kids' development, facial hair, especially eyebrows, size of snout, things like that. I suppose all you'd have to do to check if they're healthy, on the other hand, would be to feel whether their nose was wet and warm.

Sitting on my carpet that morning, feeling the sun on my face, the texture of the meditation took on an even more surreal sense. For a moment I wondered where I was; India, Canada, this world or the next. And when I filtered the information of the setting and place of this carcass through my brain I knew it was beautiful downtown Wakefield and I was happy. It felt good to remember living in this place with these trees, this river, that bridge, those streets, these people. But, it also felt good to once again realise that the differences in space, distance and time are not necessarily what we tend to think. And this time I have a lowly mouse to thank for the realisation. Only I hope that when the final dramatic experience of my enlightenment dawns, I won't dismiss it as being just a mouse trotting around my legs or the top of my head.

13. Why Did the Chicken Cross the Road?

It was just a very slow Sunday morning in March with the wrong type of weather happening, when I pulled out my 'official' papers from the drawer. There was no particular reason to look over the deed to my house again or to scrutinise the property's survey map. In truth, I don't feel any different than before I bought the place, no matter how many times I look at the papers, walk around the yard or pee on the gateposts. I keep waiting to feel more important, more puffed up or just somehow bigger, but I don't. It's not as if I'd ever just bring the fact up in conversation to impress people. The point is just that for my adult life in India I didn't have the option. As an alien, and I do love the term, I was not allowed to own property or do any business. Of course I pretended to do both, but I knew it wasn't real. Kind of like now, come to think of it.

In India, in any event, the laws actually favour the tenants. Tenants can hang on to a house for years and years while the court cases wind their way through the system. I've known cases to drag on well past the deaths of the people involved, with their offspring taking up the fight, with the owners unable to actually use their house. Sometimes all that works is to play on the superstitions of the people. One acquaintance of mine finally got some people out of his house, after about 20 years, by piling human bones on the front door-steps and hanging a skull from the overhead lamp. I've heard of a family who left their beloved home after generations only because they were being threatened with evil incantations. I suspected for some time that I was the victim of a similar scheme myself. And right or wrong it definitely worked on me.

One late night I climbed way up the hillside in the middle of a nasty rainstorm to my little rented house. The first odd thing I noticed was that the door seemed slightly ajar and, although I never locked it, I've seen enough bad movies to begin imagining the worst. So I creaked open the door, as the rain fell and thunder clapped, and slowly snuck in. I was hardly breathing as I silently made my way along the wall towards a light switch. Shadows filled the room, seemed alive at one place, then another, until with a swallow I flipped on the switch. Everything looked all right, the same as I'd left it … until my heart jumped right up into my throat. I noticed the footprints of a chicken on the floor in front of me. They were red, dripping in blood, and they were all the way up the old wooden steps to the attic room.

I'd like to say I just marched right up those steps to see what nonsense was going on up there, but the reality was quite different. I crept step-by-step up, with my chest pounding like a kettledrum, with the pulse of my temples throbbing. Step by step I forced myself to climb towards the attic until, after what felt like a long, long time, I stood on the landing with only a little light from below following me in. I was practically crying out from fear as I spotted streaks of what looked like bloodstains on the floor in front of me. I reached over and felt for the light switch, somehow finding the courage to turn the thing on. I very nearly jumped straight out of my skin when I caught sight of the dead chicken underneath an old wooden chair. I whacked my head on the cross beam even as I sped down the stairs and out the door. I was running blind along the slippery, muddy path as the rain pelted me and the thunder drove me on.

About twenty or thirty yards down the path I tripped on a rock, stumbled and landed right at the feet of a neighbour who could scare any reasonable person even in daylight. He was big and stout with an ear missing. And when I looked up at his ugly face, illuminated by lightening, he said in broken Hindi, "Have you seen my chicken?" By then I was practically out of my mind with terror. "Your chicken?', was all I could manage. "Your cat took my chicken," he said in a deep and menacing tone. I slipped around the man and carried on down the mountainside as fast as I could, never stopping, never slowing down until I reached the safety of the road. With pictures of toothless old village men and women doing strange chants around a chicken still filling my head, totally out of control potato trucks seemed far preferable. Of course, the thought did somehow filter through my panicked brain that I hadn't seen my cat all day.

Right or wrong, I never set foot in the place again. I hired someone to fetch my few belongings, and I moved to an apartment near the noisy road. Now, as I look out on a different scene in a different town, I'm feeling secure in the knowledge that I belong here, as long as it's alright with the bank, the municipality, provincial and federal governments, the neighbours, the creative intelligence, fate, karma, God in heaven . . .

14. The New Age

Having wrenched my knee playing basketball with boys half my age, but bigger and just plain better than me, was bad enough. But, to have a Reiki treatment thrust upon me made matters only worse. It made me cranky. I do believe Shelagh, a cute, twenty-year-old Australian, truly thought her healing vibrations would help me from walking sideways. She wanted to help. She was visiting the same friends I was, near here in Chelsea. Only I just dropped in for an hour and was compelled to spend the time with Shelagh's hand strategically placed on my knee.

So there we were, my boyhood friend, his wife and I, chatting as normally as can be with a very young, pretty girl sitting next to me on the couch, eyes closed tight in concentration with a hand on my knee. Discussing world politics just seemed strange under the circumstances. After at least twenty minutes she opened her eyes a couple of times and said, "There now, do you feel it?" "No", I said looking over at my old buddy, "but if you move your hand up a few inches I probably would".

Where my cynicism concerning this New Age comes from is unknown to me. There's a part of my mind, in spite of all that I've seen in my life, that remains more than sceptical in the face of Tibetan singing bowls, crystal healing, numerology, astrology, palmistry, tarot cards, sand-box therapy, Yogic flying around rooms backwards or astral travelling. I thought I astral travelled once only to discover soon after that I'd actually wet my bed. I almost had a psychic girlfriend, but she left me before we met.

I know a guy in India who's a great homeopathic doctor and one of the unhealthiest looking people you'd ever care to not meet after dark. There's a story that's been around for years about the guy, how he can't lie in the sun by the river because the vultures will think he's dead. And one of northern India's foremost psychics and 'health practitioners' is a lady who predicted the recent major earthquake. But she is so terribly overweight people suspect she may have actually caused it. Of course, I suppose it's no stranger than a one-eyed tailor or a one-armed drummer, both of which can be found in that area.

There is a lady, whose name is Mirabai, living in India who is fairly attached to her pet dog and who, obviously, was terribly upset when she thought he was so ill as to be dying. She was weeping and weeping uncontrollably, while her friends all rallied round. One of them, a lady visiting from England, said she could teach Mirabai how to find the dog again after he dies and reincarnates. She stated with some authority that she's found her same dog through five of his incarnations, the last time under a woodpile. One American fellow standing there at the time said, "Why don't you leave the poor creature alone?" I thought that was terribly clever of him.

Having said all that, however, I must add that every now and again something happens that reminds me to never close down my subjective little mind entirely. I have often felt a vague feeling of a guiding hand in my life, never stronger than as I made my way by 'chance' to Wakefield. Not long before I left India, for example, I waited in a long line to garland my teacher and couldn't help noticing that most people exchanged a few words with him during their turn. Some appeared to be having full-fledged interviews, chatting, laughing, posing with Swamiji for the camera. I noticed how each person initiated their little interactions with him, so I began to wonder what I could say. It's not usually a situation I find easy. I certainly didn't want to be the only jerk to garland him, kneeling speechless in salutation before just slithering sheepishly away.

Finally, I decided I'd simply say that he was looking especially nice and see where it would lead. As I inched towards the front of the queue I practised my sentence over and over again inside my mind. "You're looking especially nice today, Swamiji. You're looking especially nice today, Swamiji. You're looking ESPECIALLY nice today, Swamiji." It may seem slightly overdone, but I wanted the moment to go off without a hitch.

As I goose-stepped closer to the front, my sentence repeated itself in my mind almost involuntarily, more and more quickly until eventually there remained no one between us. I stepped forward with my garland; shiny purple, green and silver tinsel with its little tassel, and put it over his head. I knelt down and was about to blurt out my icebreaker when Swamiji said,

"How are your parents?" Taken quite by surprise I quickly said they were fine, a little too loudly perhaps. Then he said, "Have you heard from them lately?" I felt as though I shouted out that I'd spoken to them on the phone just recently and that they both wanted me to convey their regards. By then I was on my feet. I thought it was time to move on. Swamiji, however, then asked how my cousins were since their visit to India and I turned back even more flustered and said, "They're great. They write every day, every week, I mean every month or so". Then I began moving away when I heard Swamiji call out to me, "By the way, you're looking especially nice today."

On the eve of the SEP Psychic Exposition at the Ottawa Congress Centre, which I intend to check out and report back to our reader about, I offer these observations only in order to bring this great New Age into perspective. And you can believe me when I say that there's a lot I don't know. I don't know how to drink a lot of booze without turning into a moron. I don't know how to change a spark plug, or go dog sledding, shoot a moose or stuff a beaver, so to speak. But, in the field of mysticism, spirituality and meditation, I know a little bit. And what I want to say today is that, if at all one wants to be a great sage, I believe the matter simply has everything to do with love.

15. Flying

Looking at myself in the airplane's bathroom mirror, I could see hair growing from my ears. Lots of it. And I decided right then and there that I had to stop drinking so much of this strong western coffee.

I was obviously in shock, again. Last week I was working the night shift at Ryan's Famous Garage and Towing Company in Alcove, and this week I headed for Los Angeles to housesit a mansion in the Hollywood Hills. Forget India. How long can I milk this twenty-three years in India thing anyway? Now I miss Wakefield.

I'd been asked to watch over some renovations for a friend of mine in LA while he went to India. He also is a writer; only he makes actual money at it. Muchos dineros. I played Jo Dee Messina's 'Silver Thunderbird' on my car's tape deck over and over and over all the way to Toronto. Bopping along, grooving to lines like, "Forget your Eldorado. The foreign car's absurd. If there's a God up in heaven, he's driving a silver Thunderbird," as I zipped along in my trusty little gold Toyota. Five or six hours absolutely rocking to the tune changed dramatically, of course, as soon as I entered my parents' apartment, where traditionally it takes ten minutes to butter a piece of toast. Just as I cross the threshold it's as though I've stepped into an aquarium, and I just have to pray there's enough oxygen to go around.

A day and a half later, as I checked in for my flight, I soulfully asked the attendant if she might upgrade me to the Business Class section. I told her about my poor dead aunt and how I had a fourteen-hour nightmare drive from the upper Gatineau mountains, how I hit a moose, how I could look forward to another ten-hour drive after the flight to get to the funeral on time. I pointed out that I was only one single fellow, that I always fly American Airlines and have never asked before. Yes, of course it was a pack of bold-faced lies, but the very kindly looking lady listened patiently and said that the plane was overbooked, but she'd do whatever she could for me.

As I passed through the gate, from out of some hidden heavenly realm, an attendant walked up, scribbled something on my ticket and announced that I'd been placed in Business Class. Everyone stood up and clapped. Well not really, but needless to say I was vociferous in my thanks and I vaguely remember asking if he wanted his shoes polished. For the first time in my life the dead aunt thing worked. I was in Business Class. My seat was deep and cushiony, with armrests big enough to seat a half dozen Himalayan villagers. I had my own television screen, and the stewardesses were very friendly. The fellow on my right was busy with his laptop, and the fellow on my left was using his calculator; so I pretended to read the stock market report.

I couldn't figure out how to put my seat into a reclining position and eventually concluded it just didn't recline. I felt a terrific pang of disappointment. Then I couldn't figure out how to turn the television off even though the channels wouldn't change and my neighbour's was off. I didn't want to let on that I was new to the business class, so instead of asking I continued to read the newspaper while watching the people around me.

Eventually, I noticed one or two seats go back into what looked like awfully comfortable positions, so I just had to ask my right-hand neighbour. Eventually, I also asked my left-hand neighbour how to turn the television off, and he said they don't shut off until after the safety instructions. "But yours is off," I blundered. He chuckled rather smugly, I thought, and pointed out that it only looked off from my angle of vision. After take-off we were directed to open our trays. Mine didn't seem to work. The attendant came over looking frustrated with my ineptitude and opened it with embarrassing ease.

By that time I felt like standing on top of my soft seat and yelling, "yes, this is in fact my first time in Business Class, and I'm a bumbling plebeian who's supposed to be in the cattle cars with the rest of my people. One day, however, we will rise up and take over this part of the plane! We'll tear out the trays, the televisions and the seats, throw the silver tea service all about, and snatch the individualised toilet packs with their toothbrushes, toothpaste, dental floss, face and hand cream, washcloth and shaving equipment."

At the end of the flight the tourist class passengers disembarked first, which I thought a little odd until the announcement was made that the plane was landing in five minutes. Wait for me, Wakefield.

16. Modern Times

Walking through the badlands of Los Angeles has done little to make me think I've made any mistake in judging where the right place for me in this western world would be. Wakefield still rules. And roaming the halls and balconies of this house only serves to reinforce that sense. Nice place to visit, of course, but one single guy just does not need five bathrooms. Nobody's digestion is that bad. And why, I find myself asking, does the owner of this establishment, who happens to be almost completely bald, need four hair dryers? Why does he need a bathtub the size of my living room back there in Wakefield?

The strength and power of the toilet's flush system is awesome. It's lucky I'm the kind of guy that stands up before flushing or I might've ended up in China, and my allegiance is with the Tibetans. One flush like that back home and I'd have to call the kindly Mr Carol Dubois of Les Services Sanitaires. I have a holding tank, after all. In India, of course, I'd be lucky to have a latrine that flushed at all. For many years I had to pour a bucket of water down the thing in order to make the world all right.

Traditionally, the villagers went for a rather long walk each morning with a tumbler of water to take care of the whole matter, just in case you had always wanted to know. One very early and misty morning, years ago, our bus rolled into the famous holy town of Brindawan, the birthplace of lord Krishna. After searching feverishly and unsuccessfully for a latrine, my buddy, a lawyer from Vancouver, asked my advice. I suggested a long walk across a nearby field. I handed him a bottle of water. He looked at the bottle, and then he looked at me as if to say, 'why did I ever agree to this trip,' before trundling off over hill and dale.

I doubt that he felt the spiritual qualities of the place just then, and not for some time to come, as it turned out. Several minutes after sending him off to do his business, I spotted him rushing back, his face a mask of terror. When I asked what happened, he spluttered out a story of how, no sooner had he rid himself of all of yesterday, so to speak, that a whole herd of ravenous pigs stampeded straight at him in order to be the first in line for breakfast. And so it was that my friend learned first hand how the sanitation system used to work in village India, and evidently still does to some extent.

Now here in Los Angeles, no such problem exists, at least not in Hollywood. Of course, I've had a couple of bad moments when I've had to get to a latrine in a hurry only to find that I was required to fumble around for a quarter to get in. And that's not such an easy thing to do under pressure. In contrast to my shower in Wakefield, with its pathetic little stream of somewhat brackish water, the one here in the master bathroom has two strategically placed showerheads, each with a near perfect flow of water. The bathtub, however, is something else entirely. Large enough for several water buffalo to keep cool in during the summer heat, it sports a mosaic tile floor and sides with a built-in Jacuzzi. The first time I used the thing I nearly drowned. And I only figured out how to use the Jacuzzi yesterday.

I've gotten into the habit of pouring in copious amounts of something I found here called, 'Peaches and Cream Moisturising Foam Bath.' Please understand that until recently in India one has had to take most of a morning to heat up a bucket of water to use for bathing. One would kneel down in front of it as in worship while ladling its precious liquid over ones head and shoulders. Therefore, you can understand my taking to the tub here in LA like, well, a fish to water. Yesterday, however, after nearly falling asleep while soaking in the tub and watching MTV at the same time, I began to fiddle with the switches, as I've often done before during this last week. I nearly jumped right up the marble wall when one switch miraculously activated the jet streams of the Jacuzzi. Settling down and sitting back against one of the outpourings of bubbled water, I couldn't for the life of me understand what was so great about it. At the same time, all the 'Peaches and Cream' foam began to make huge amounts of suds under the pressure of the jet streams, to such an extent that it very nearly began to spill out into the room before I could figure out how to stop the thing.

Lastly, I have yet to figure out what the purpose of that somewhat smaller toilet-like fixture is. It appeared to turn on and off normally as I leaned over the thing until, with the flip of one switch, it sprayed me right in the face.

17. *Los Angeles all Over*

Sitting at Starbucks' coffee shop in Hollywood yesterday, it was all I could do to keep my thoughts to myself. And I was alone. It just seems to me that this is a whole society of inordinately large-breasted, suspiciously thin women, mostly blonde.

I don't mind admitting that remarks like, 'Oh for heaven's sake,' 'jimminy cricket,' and 'dear Jesus son of God,' kept leaping to mind with such power that I almost found myself asking the counter-person for some counselling to go with my muffin and cappuccino. Even the old ladies have big, perfect bazoomas. I saw one ancient lady using a walker yesterday with a huge set that stood up straighter than billboards. I can only assume this phenomenon has something to do with the orange juice here.

Needless to say, Sunset Boulevard or Ventura Boulevard is somewhat of a contrast to hanging out at Ryan's Garage. When a lovely lady drove up to the station back home my nose would be firmly pressed to the window of the big garage doors pretty much straight away. I almost broke my nose on one occasion. Nevertheless, I tell you honestly that the ladies back home are more real and more attractive than what I've seen in this neck of the woods. It's just the sheer volume, which I mean in more than one way, that becomes a bit of a hazard here, especially as I drive along in my buddy's Lexus looking to all the world like a big time player. It's been tricky to stay out of the back seats of cars ahead of me, as I twist my neck again and again to see if what I saw could possibly have been what I saw. I saw a young, thin lady, for example, with a rack on her that would make the folks at Pritchard's dairy farm jealous. I'm sure she could feed a small orphanage in New Delhi with those udders, practically dragging on the sidewalk as they were. I've even seen nice breasts on a few guys here.

One time, when I was in Bombay on business, an acquaintance insisted upon taking me to what I thought was a nightclub, but which I discovered was in fact the Indian equivalent of a strip joint. A lady, who looked as though she really would've been better employed at home picking lice out of her baby's hair, danced terribly to some of the worst live music I've ever heard. She wore a two-piece costume that showed a bit of her midriff and shoulders. It was made of that shiny, colourful tinsel that Indians use to decorate their houses and temples during each of their multitudinous celebrations; she never took any part of her costume off, thank heaven. The climax of the show was when she made her way around the room shaking hands with each man in the place, but she somehow cosmically missed me. It was as if the creative intelligence was saying, 'you're not really meant to be here.'

On a shimmering and sun-filled true Californian afternoon this week, I sat half in the car munching down a Burrito and watching the world's beautiful people rush inexorably on towards God knows what. Two perfect specimens strolled by. They were the classic tall, thin and blonde types that man has for some reason or other decided is the best the species has to offer. They had unnaturally large breasts busting out all over, and it occurred to me that they must save a bundle on clothes because there wasn't much on them to speak of. And they each gave me the nicest, warmest smiles I've had since my mother saw me in a rodeo. I was eleven years old and riding an agreeable little pony called 'Butterball.' At first it occurred to me that the two chicks thought I was really cool, as I choked on a bean, until I realised it was the car. They actually stopped to chat; you can imagine how enjoyable it was for me, when we got to the inevitable question of my vocation, to tell them proudly that I'm a gas station attendant. If they had looked any more deflated I'm sure their breasts would've begun to shrink right before my eyes.

Having said all of that, I should really add that I'm having a great time. I've met some good people, eaten some good food; I even had a small role in a movie offered to me. I had to turn it down, though, because the director insisted I get something called implants. Call me old fashioned, but that just isn't me.

18. The Postman Always Rings Twice

There were rarely line-ups at the post office where I lived in India. It was worse than that. At every wicket groups of people with varying degrees of personal hygiene would crowd in, haphazardly, jostling for position. It was during those moments of trying to box out the tough, scrappy villagers that I appreciated my training as a basketball player and the sage advice of my high-school coach: "Kill! Kill! Kill!"

The large, cavernous post office was an unpainted, cement affair about a half-hour walk from my place. One had to take care to reach it at a proper time. There were lunch-hour shutdowns and tea breaks, designated times for registering letters and packages with regular shortages of international shtumps. I remember an occasion when it took at least twenty minutes to finally break through the swollen crowd to buy shtumps, only to be told by the clerk, with an engaging smile, that it was time for his tea break. While he mindlessly slurped his hot tea by pouring it from cup onto the saucer in order to lap it up, I was being mashed into the counter by the hordes, my face pressed against the iron bars of the wicket. When the fellow finally returned he didn't have any shtumps.

I've experienced countless shortages of shtumps, sometimes being reduced to plastering copious amounts of lesser ones all over my epistle, leaving the address barely discernible. There was also the matter of finding a way to get the envelopes to stay closed or the shtumps to stay stuck to the envelope. For that purpose the office supplied dirt-encrusted brown plastic containers with a hint of paste on the bottom and a short stick for application. Security was a problem. When sending a letter you'd always want to see the clerk actually shtump the shtump to be sure it wasn't taken off and pocketed by a grossly underpaid public servant.

Letters and packages regularly arrived open, inspected, picked over. Several years before leaving, at a time when a few extra roupees would've really come in handy, I received a birthday card from my parents. The card had a picture of a horse on it, a touching poem and my mom had written, "Spend this money wisely." I tore the envelope apart looking for a cheque or cash, Canadian tire money, anything. I searched the ground beneath my feet and the garbage bucket. Nothing. I never got that money.

It has been said that a visit to an Indian post office is equivalent to several years with a true guru for the attainment of enlightenment. Anyway, I just said it. Several visits will ensure deep insights into the human condition, as well as understanding, patience and an inherent ability to 'go with the flow'. I would recommend a trip to the bus station to just finish off the whole process if you were really serious about self-realisation. I believe, however, that one way or another it's the same all over the world.

Driving my buddy's Lexus to the post office down here on Beverly Street in Beverly Hills, California, was easy enough. In fact, I felt good. The traffic was light. Having parked, I walked across the street to the office and in through the sliding doors of a lovely light-blue room with plants and paintings, but had to wait in an incredibly long line. Hardly a few moments later, however, I remembered I forgot to put a quarter in the parking meter, and by the time I scooted back to the car it was too late. Whatever official person is in charge of finding deadbeats like me must've been lurking in a nearby doorway, prepared to pounce quickly. My little trip to the post office would cost a minimum of thirty U. S. dollars.

Back at the post office, the line up was as long as it was orderly. People shifted from one foot to the other as they shuffled bit by bit between the ropes, inching towards their future without a complaint. I noticed several people talking on cell phones, so I took one that I had out of my shoulder bag. It was my friend's phone. I had never received a call on it nor had I ever called anyone. It had also long since run out of battery power, but I pretended to carry on a conversation anyway, even laughing once for effect. A little oriental lady finally reached the front of the line with her parcel, only to be told by an uncaring clerk behind the Plexiglas window that she had to go away and come back after she labelled the package in a different fashion. At first, due to a language problem, the oriental lady didn't understand. Once she did understand, however, we could all see that she was practically in tears as she walked away. And then a very, very large African-American lady near the front, whom nobody was going to mess with, called out in a big, booming voice "Yo!! Y'all just come right on over here, little sister! Yo not goin' to the back of no lineup! I got me a big ol' marker here, and we gonna do this thing together!"

19. Venice Beach

Without there being too many days left for me in Los Angeles, I decided to head out to Venice beach. It was a long drive, though one done as though in a trance, drawn to the place by the overpowering magnetic force of its reputation. I parked in an underground parking lot. I remembered my friend telling me to always park in covered and/or supervised lots to protect his expensive Lexus from riffraff. It made me feel slightly uneasy because I suspected the riffraff he was referring to would probably be my buddies were I to live there. Of course, if I went to the beach in my little '87 Tercel, well, I'd just stick it any old place. Or, better still, I could walk to that spot under the famous Wakefield covered bridge and do my doggie paddling nearly in my own backyard. I couldn't do it right in my own backyard because my mom always said I should keep my fingernails clean. How one presents oneself is so important, she used to say while lighting one cigarette off another. I get a little choked up as I recall her telling me, just as though it were yesterday, "Nathan," she would say, "if you don't stop being such a dirty little bastard, you're going to end up looking like one of those awful people from India." But, I digress.

There's nothing quite like Venice Beach and, more specifically, the place they call Muscle Beach. It was my good luck to arrive while tryouts were being held for a new television show called, 'Battle Dome'. The name alone should go a long way toward telling you what the tryouts were like and what the show will be like. Hopefuls were required to climb a rope as fast as they could, do as many push ups as they could, run as fast as they could, and look as mean and animalistic as they possibly could. Whoever could climb the fastest, do the most push ups, run the fastest and look the most demonic presumably would win parts on the show. Most of the guys as well as some of the girls were quite reptilian looking, like creatures from out of Star Wars. Some may well have had parts in Jurassic Park. Can you spell 'steroids'? Some really should've been released into the rain forest somewhere, but instead at least a few of them were about to become highly paid television stars.

The section of the tryouts I enjoyed the most was when each of the Battle Dome aspirants had to stand in front of a camera, flex their over-sized muscles and rant on about how they were going to destroy, pulverise, annihilate and perhaps eat their enemies. It was hard to move on from Muscle Beach and the tryouts. And yet, there seemed so much to see and so little time. I wasn't used to being away from the Jacuzzi for so long.

The next area I came to was the basketball courts. There were three full-sized courts, and they were all busy with some really good quality talent. In one intense game, a rather lanky fellow ran the length of the court, while I watched, for what turned out to be a backward slam-dunk. And all the way back to his end he kept hollering "Its just too pretty! It's just too pretty!" In the schoolyard near where I lived in India there was a beautiful, full-sized basketball court also. It had Fibreglass backboards, recessed poles and proper hoops and nets also. The only problem was that the masons, in their eagerness to do an 'export-quality' job, finished off the court with a glazed coating of pure cement instead of leaving it plain asphalt. In finishing off a house that meant the contractor was doing a top-notch job. In finishing off a basketball court that meant the players slipped and slid all over the place. That meant nobody could stop and nobody could shoot. The net result has been a generation of athletes playing a game of something in between basketball and West Quebec broomball.

Along the boardwalk at Venice Beach there were more psychics and palm readers than I've ever seen in one place. There were tattoo artists and cheap jewellery stalls along with the usual funky dresses, baseball caps and posters. For me, however, the most striking feature of that part of the beach was the hawkers and vendors, who looked as if they'd been sitting there twirling their hemp ropes and designing their candles since the sixties. When I couldn't walk another step I sat on a bench beside a cute, young girl wearing a halter-top and bell-bottoms. She had sparkles on her eyes, and I had the distinct impression I may have known her mother thirty years earlier. She did not look too happy and eventually asked if I had seen her rabbit.

"Excuse me?" I asked.

"I've lost my rabbit."

"I'm sorry," I said as sincerely as possible under the circumstances. "I haven't noticed one around here."

"He's a Sagittarius."

I assured her I'd keep my eyes open for him. And then I carried on back to the parking lot.

20. Cats: The Play

In this large, terraced house overlooking Hollywood, I actually occupy only one small room. It's not the nicest bedroom by far. The nicest, the master bedroom, has hardwood floors and French doors that lead out to the terrace and show a view of the skyline. It sports a walk-in closet the size of my living room in Wakefield and a sofa like quicksand. I go there. I visit. But I dwell on the other side of the house in a room where I can hear the neighbours and especially the neighbour's cat. I enjoy hearing the cat in the night. In fact, I listen for his or her sounds when I'm in bed. She or he won't come near me, but I still enjoy seeing it cross the window as I watch television of an evening. Then at least I know some other creature actually lives around here. For the past few days, however, I've been convinced the little feline's been coming inside the house.

I'm supposed to keep the doors all closed, locked and use the air-conditioning with the alarm system on, but of course I don't. I keep all the doors wide open. There's nothing particularly valuable here anyway. The home entertainment system, with the screen that comes down from the ceiling, with its huge projector hanging up there, and all those consoles in the wall cabinet can't be worth much. There's a lot of useless-looking though admittedly shiny jewellery and stuff in the wall safe. He has several VCRs and he's got old statues and paintings that really can't be worth anything to speak of. Of course, I'd miss the computer.

For the past few days, as I've sat at this computer, with its 12.5 gigabytes, whatever that means, I kept hearing a cat. I'd get up and walk around the room, look under tables, even up the fake fireplace until I finally realised the meowing was coming from the computer! Whenever I had an incoming message, a cat's meowing would sound over the speakers to let me know. That means that every time a message from a friend had arrived, I had been jumping up and wandering around the rooms hoping to catch a glimpse of the neighbour's pussy. In my own defence I must point out that my faithful plodder of a computer back in Wakefield doesn't even have speakers.

Cats in India, by and large, are not appreciated. In fact, they're vilified. They're considered by many to be downright evil. And yet, at one point I had three. At the same time my buddy, Doctor John, was having a big problem with mice. As a Vietnam War veteran, John did have a few eccentricities and a few issues. On one occasion, when a truck backfired near where we sat at an outside café, he jumped right under the table. I had to lean over and convince him that the Viet Cong had gone back into the jungle. He hankered after a charming cottage in a rather secluded village, and the fellow moving from there, Randy, wanted to be first paid for a few of the improvements he'd made. Randy and John came to an impasse and asked me to arbitrate. During the discussion that followed things got ugly. Randy turned to me and asked if I thought he was being unreasonable. I said, "I really don't know, Randy, but the doctor here's beginning to look at you like you're the enemy." For some reason or another that line seemed to do the trick. They were able to get past the negotiations, and Doctor John moved in. He turned a lovely place into something that resembled a bunker, with high rock walls, and barbed wire; and he kept the curtains drawn most of the time. And he had mice.

One morning, around that period of time, I drove up to Doctor John's cottage and presented him with the solution to his problem. I handed him a young cat. He was very grateful and full of hope as he cradled the little critter in his arms. A couple of weeks later I again drove out there for a visit, and the Doctor happily announced that he hadn't had a single mouse since I gave him the cat. I couldn't help noticing, however, the cat's food dish outside the cottage rather than inside. I asked about that and Doctor John said, "Oh, I keep him outside." Naturally, I asked how keeping the cat outside would have any effect on the mouse problem inside. So then the good Doctor leaned over and snatched the cat. "Here's how it works," he said. He carried the cat into the cottage and proceeded to rub it all over the counters, chairs, even the carpets and floorboards. Then he tossed it unceremoniously back outside. And throughout it all the cat looked as though it was all in an honest day's work.

Needless to say, this house in the Hollywood hills does not have a mouse problem. Exterminators come once a week to make sure nothing survives. Now I find it doesn't even have a cat problem. And soon it won't have a Nathan problem 'cause I'm moving on to Vancouver. In fact, I'm moving toward Wakefield. I just have to put the final touches to my tan and then I'll pack.

21. *Flying Home*

Tooling around the gulf islands off the coast of British Columbia's been like a pilgrimage. It all started here for me. Nanaimo, Qualicum Beach and even Gabriola Island, though more populated, seemed largely as they had been in the early 1970s. On Gabriola, there was the same road wrapping the island, the same marina, shops and farms. There were the same places I'd lived. Even that strange geodesic dome, where I first hung my bandanna, was there.

Having arrived on Gabriola Island without a pot to you-know-what-in, some people I knew for a matter of hours offered me their unfinished dome to camp out in for the winter while they went east to visit their families. In lieu of rent I was only required to take care of their beautiful snow white German shepherd, named Blacky. Blacky was incredibly skinny. My friends, being passionately vegetarian themselves, obviously wanted theirs to be the world's first granola-crunching dog. But, he was positively skeletal. So when I was alone in the dome with my new friend the first thing I decided to do was canter down to the island grocery store and pick up a nice, big, fat slab of something that used to run and jump, for Blacky's dinner. I looked forward to the pleasure of watching him eat it.

That night we feasted together, Blacky and I; he on his meat and me on my tofu. One of us went wild. While I munched away in a civilised, peaceful, almost meditative fashion, my alter ego ripped apart that steak near-by. We bonded. The way he looked at me was truly gratifying. I knew I'd made a friend for life, which as it turned out was not very long. Having had the taste of blood for the first time in a dog's age, Blacky just couldn't quite settle down. He just couldn't wait for the can of juicy, meaty Ken-L-Rations that was on the menu for his culinary pleasure that night. He went after the neighbour's chickens and was shot to death for his trouble.

It was a peaceful winter. Eventually, I wrote to tell my friends that

Blacky had wandered off and not returned. They firmly believed that Blacky had set out for Ontario to find them. Apparently one of them had a dream to that effect. Walking through Kitsilano in Vancouver opened me up to more and different memories that flooded in somewhat unexpectedly. I remembered lounging in Banyan Books when there was a loft for people like me to meditate in. The Naam was a funkier, more laid back kind of vegetarian restaurant. There were no cyber cafes. And as I strolled down Fourth Avenue I felt as though I was floating back in time.

The year was 1975 when I walked into Lifestream restaurant on a bright August afternoon and spotted a poster announcing a three-day meditation retreat with Ruth Dennison. I hadn't thought of joining a Vipassana retreat at all for quite some time. But I'd been fond of Ruth Dennison, an elderly, gracious lady who was one of only four teachers in the world designated by U Ba Kin of Rangoon, Burma. It struck me as odd that the retreat was called for only three days. All Vipassana retreats were supposed to be ten days long or multiples therein. I'd heard that Ruth was getting herself into hot water with Goenka and Mother Siama, the two main leaders of the group, for making a few changes in the strict regimen of the retreats, and I supposed that was the change.

The first day of the retreat was very much the same as many other times. We were silent as before. We ate the same and listened to the same instructions as I remembered. But then, in the middle of the second day, Ruth asked us to get up and walk onto the lawn. That alone surprised me. When she instructed us to fly around the yard like butterflies I was positively shocked. A flood of thoughts poured through my mind in a moment. 'How dare she! I've not been meditating five years to be made a fool of! That's so undignified! It's not Vipassana! I can't! I won't!' At the same time everyone else began to flit about so I really had very little choice. I spread my wings reluctantly and began to slowly flutter around, but as soon as I did I exploded with laughter. I began to fly like a butterfly, higher than an eagle, laughing and fluttering and soaring. I spread my wings as I glided faster until I crash-landed in a paroxysm of laughter on the green grass.

I haven't seen Ruth Dennison in over twenty years now. I heard somewhere along the way that she had been kind of excommunicated, but not before she'd taught at least one very serious student of life how to fly. And now I'm flying home to Wakefield.

22. *Dad*

There are certain precious moments in time one remembers forever, moments so dramatic, touching and meaningful that they shape one's life. The moments I'm about to describe are not like that at all. These moments were much too normal and banal to be of any consequence. Still, I kinda liked them. They concern my old dad, the judge.

A friend collected me at the airport upon my arrival back in Toronto, thereby saving dad the drive, not to mention any undue stress to other motorists who happened to be out just at that time on that stretch of road. As soon as I entered my parents' apartment, after hugs, kisses and pinches, we sat down in the den, and they remarked on my nicely shortened hair and beard. My dad launched into his proverbial dissertation on the marvels of the modern electric shaver. In fact, he insisted I at least look at his. He went to bring it out from the bathroom as I peered over at mom. She couldn't help me. No one could. Dad stood in the middle of the den shaving, telling me that I might not like it at first, but would soon wonder how I'd ever gotten along without it.

"David, he's not interested," my mom tried to say over the sound of the thing.

"You see this part under the chin?" he called over to me, "This is the trickiest part. You have to pass over it a few extra times."

"David, if you get hairs on the rug I'll kill you," barked mom.

"Whadya talkin' bout? This shaver doesn't drop hairs!"

'Oh for heavens sake, David, put it away!"

When he came back into the den, dad sat in his chair with the Obus-form backrest and offered the shaver to me free of charge. I didn't really respond so he started in on my future plans.

"Are you going to ask for a substantial raise from that newspaper of yours? What's the circulation? Find out the circulation and let me know."

Next day, I watched him scour the menu of a local restaurant. It was not a pretty sight. He'd been instructed by his doctor to stay right away from bread, but to eat rice-cakes instead. And that's like suggesting that a junkie switch to Tylenol. The well-meaning waitress had no way of knowing she shouldn't have put the bread basket right in front of him. In our haste to clear it from dad's line of vision, mom and I both grabbed at the basket sending several fresh buns bouncing onto his lap as he just looked at us stoically.

It's a sign of my father's age that he's being allowed less and less of the food and activities he loves. I can so far only imagine what it must feel like. But, during those rain-soaked days in Toronto it was clear to me that soon he'll have to give up driving as well. I've known for some time that to go in the car with dad was to tax my nerves beyond their natural limits. I have no idea when he stopped looking behind for other cars before switching lanes. Many have been the times I've witnessed overwrought drivers, having swerved to narrowly miss us cutting in front of them, shaking fists. And he, with an expression of total incomprehension written all over his face, would exclaim "What the hell's the matter with them?" Many have been the times when I've coaxed him to go when he was wrongly stopped, stop when he was not supposed to go, pleaded with him to stay in his lane, begged him unsuccessfully to give me the wheel.

Returning from the restaurant, as lunch sat uneasily in my stomach after the drive, we pulled up in front of the underground garage to the apartment. Dad stopped on the slope leading down to the door to switch glasses. He pushed the button to activate the garage door and as it swung open he fished around for his clear glasses. "Now where the dickens are they?" he said, becoming more and more frustrated. "Oh for heaven's sake!" Of course, by the time he finally located his glasses the door had closed again, just as we began rolling down towards it.

"Dad, stop," I yelled

"What?"

"Dad, stop."

"What are you saying?"

"Stop!"

"David, stop the car!!!" mom hollered. That did it, of course, as he somehow, miraculously, came to a sudden halt inches from the closed garage door. "Oh for Pete's sake," he exclaimed at no one in particular. "You'd think with all the money we pay for the upkeep of this building they could fix this blasted door." I'm reminded of how my folks had to disallow my old granddad from driving way back when I was barely old enough to sit atop my tricycle. And I know one day it'll be my turn.

The morning I left for Wakefield was teeming with rain, and mom didn't want me to go. Dad took my side and even offered to drive me to where my car was sitting at my brother's place, but I thought better of it. I took the bus. In a way, I'm always sorry to leave them. And I've never been able to figure out why I always sleep so well there. In spite of our being worlds apart in so many ways, mom's cigarettes, dad's shaver, I feel at home wherever they are. "Phone when you arrive," was the last thing I heard my mom say as I closed the apartment door. And I suppose that's just about the way it's supposed to be.

23. No Place Like Home

Back in 1975 you could still cross more or less unhindered through countries like Iran and Afghanistan. During that fall, I rode the mysterious Orient Express to Greece and the whimsical magic bus through Turkey. Passing the Indian frontier, I felt the excitement of a long-cherished dream about to be realised, an excitement not the least diminished by the British boy, seated across, who insisted he'd lost his stomach in India. I assumed he was returning to look for it, and I paid no heed.

Practically the first sight to meet my eyes on the crowded streets of Amritsar was of two men beating a water buffalo with clubs. After a few moments of indecision and a further few minutes of dithering, I walked up decisively and pulled both men off the buffalo, pushed one to the ground and grabbed his club. I yelled and threatened them with a similar beating until, after the initial shock had worn off, they grabbed the buffalo's rope in unison and handed it to me saying something that probably meant, "Fine! This huge creature who eats tons of food and refuses to work is now yours." I didn't want the buffalo. I just wanted them to behave in a civilised manner. But my ego impelled me to snatch the rope defiantly and curse them roundly as they walked away as though they hadn't a care in the world.

So, after being in India for hardly a half-hour I was walking through Amritsar looking for the holy Golden Temple, leading a mammoth and, I was soon to discover, singularly stubborn water buffalo around by a rope. I doubted the city had an 'adopt-a-pet' program, and the more I coaxed him further on, the more she or he resisted, until I felt like beating the medieval monster. Eventually, in the second evening, a sadarji dressed in the blue courte pyjama and orange turban of a khalistani freedom fighter, whose name was Harjit, after listening to my story took pity on me. "Coming along then, Mr Nathan," he sang out as he grabbed my free hand."You most certainly did the right thing, but still you're hanging on the situation, isn't it?"

Together, the three of us walked to the edge of town where Harjit led us inside a tree-lined field, and there he took out the buffalo's nose ring, whacked its rump and sent it waddling off happily into the field and me into India.

By way of contrast, my entry into Wakefield, the virtual village, was less dramatic, though no less significant I believe. Having come for one night, I seriously fell in love with the place. But, alas, I was promised to another; Toronto. At the very point of my departure, however, I wrenched my back severely. I could only shuffle, like something people choose from a tank at seafood restaurants, to be plopped into the next available pot of boiling water. It happened while visiting my friend, Lori, who was house-sitting at the pottery studio and home of David, Maureen and charming Annie and Allegro (not their real names of course). The house was full of some of the most artistic, pleasing and well-executed ceramic creations it's ever been my pleasure to see up close. And I saw a lot of it over the next several days because I lay where I fell, so to speak.

During the second afternoon of my injury, while Lori was away looking for napkins to wipe my chin with, I decided to try and make it to the sun-drenched front yard. There was a canvas chair calling my name. Little by little, sliding one foot at a time forward, with the family pooch running excitedly around me with a stick in its mouth, I inched toward that chair. After what felt like a trek to the base camp at Mount Everest, I arrived. Of course, I had to position myself in such a manner that my backside was aiming straight at the seat so that, when I allowed myself to fall back, I'd land in the chair. Having satisfied myself that I was on-course, I fell backwards but the old canvas snapped under the force of my derriere and I went 'fump,' right down through the struts of the contraption. It gave new meaning to the expression, 'my ass was in a sling.'

At first I was in so much pain and frustration that I cursed in a fashion reserved only for special occasions. Eventually, I just tipped myself over and wriggled out onto the grass where I lay motionless, except for my right arm, which I utilised for the purpose of tossing a stick for the dog. Right then and there I decided to make the town my home. I know a cosmic happening when I see one.

24. Outbreak

The last time I took a plane from India, nothing particularly unusual happened. We went up. We came down. The large lady beside me hogged the armrest. The man on the other side snored into my ear. The dessert of my vegetarian meal was fruit cup while everyone else got carrot cake with icing. The time before, however, was quite different.

On that flight, the airline showed a scary film about a horrible plague brought to America via a man bitten by an infected monkey in deepest Africa. The man fell deathly ill, sweating, delirious, on a Trans-Atlantic flight to San Francisco. Although Dustin Hoffman saved the country and his marriage by the end, it was a case of too little too late for the guy on that plane. And it wasn't pretty.

Now, hardly forty minutes after the end of the flick, we touched down at London's Heathrow airport, but were not allowed to disembark. We waited and waited until everyone was fidgety, irritable and ready to bark. When the captain finally got on the blower to explain the delay, what he said did little to alleviate the tension throughout the cabin. He told us that a man had fallen deathly ill, sweating, delirious on the flight, and health officials were on the way to inspect him.

No one dared mention anything about the eerie coincidence. Of course, in the film people began dropping like flies pretty much right away. So we kept looking around to see if anyone fell out into the isle. A fellow across from me looked like he might suffer an aneurysm any moment, but otherwise everyone seemed like a normal bunch of mildly freaked out folks.

Eventually, of course, we were let off, without quarantine. No men in space suits filtered down through the rows of seats. But I, for one, made a mental note to inquire as to what film was scheduled before booking my next flight. I mean, if it was to be one in which a plane crashed in mountains and the survivors are reduced to eating their dead, I'd be inclined to rethink my itinerary.

I recently began some house painting with Mr Tony Picard of Picard Enterprises. And if you wanna re-affirm that some people still take pride in their work, just tag along with Tony for a few days. He asked if I was an experienced painter and, needless to say, I insisted I was. After all, I had worked as a painter for quite some time. Unfortunately, that had been over twenty-eight years back; while the wrist action was still good, Tony soon realised I needed to seriously brush up on my technique, excuse the expression. He asked if I'd ever done any scraping, and I said I'd been scraping most of my life.

Nevertheless, I found myself slathering on the primer in a Chelsea cottage one recent misty morning and listening to not-so-Magic 100 on my little radio. It seems to me that the most profound advancement in radio listening, during the more than two decades I'd been away, has been the thirty minutes of uninterrupted music without advertisements. They advertise that fact incessantly, of course, along with the radio's call letters. They repeat, ad nauseam, their motto of not so hard and not so soft, which always reminds me of the last time I . . . oh never mind.

Someone was singing about leaving someone for someone better when I began to also hear the ominous sound of a loudspeaker in the distance, getting louder by the minute. In India, that usually meant trouble of some sort. And I'm sorry to say I couldn't understand the French being called out, but my imagination went into overdrive. I was working alone that day and hadn't seen another human being for hours. Then I spotted five men all dressed in bright orange space suits approach from out of the woods.

My first thought was of the movie I'd seen on that flight from India. My next thought was about becoming an organ donor; probably because the subject has been beaten to death, pardon the expression, in the news lately. I'm not sure I'd be doing anyone any great favour, especially the poor sucker who got my liver, but it didn't come to that. When our eyes met, the leader of the group called out in English that they were clearing brush from hydro lines and were wondering simply if they could turn their truck around in the yard.

25. Monkey Business

In retrospect I can see how odd it was to have finally arrived in India only to go into retreat almost immediately for a month. And after concluding that retreat, at the Tibetan Library of Works and Archives in the village of McCloud Ganj, I merely shifted to the Toshiba Retreat Centre. That's where I came to know the habits of monkeys because the place was lousy with them. In between recitations of my mantra and nibbling away at my meals, I basically found myself meditating on their fighting, eating and lovemaking. And while 'love making' is a term that may be applicable for some procreating humans, at least I like to think so as regards my family, it's a stretch when describing what monkeys do.

They're quite clever at times. If I'd leave any article of clothing out on a line unattended, it'd be snatched up by one or another of the sly simian creatures within a moment and held for ransom. One banana could get me my shoe back. A mango would secure the release of a book only slightly damaged. I recall their frustration with a tremendous sense of satisfaction, however, when I offered no reward whatsoever for a pair of undies they'd pilfered. Let them keep the undies, I said to myself.

For the next many years I continued to study the monkey mind, learning how to free it from its natural confines. I'm not one of those folks who smugly talk about how the human race hasn't progressed much since the days we spent most of our time in trees, if at all you subscribe to that theory. On the contrary, I believe there's a sub-culture swelling in the body of the populace that has prayed, meditated or contemplated upon the fact that we are all one essential energy, light or life. Which is not to say there isn't still a tendency, nasty at times, towards a misunderstanding of that subtle sameness.

In the peculiar jungle of Internet chat rooms, for example, people are willing, and in fact feel quite free, to share their most intimate secrets with total strangers. Things they wouldn't tell their parish priests they're willing to tell me, a guy who's named himself, for the purpose of those chat rooms at least, after a Toyota. There's the example of Highandry, whom I met in a room called 'Open Arms, Warm Hearts.' We got to chatting, one thing led to another, and after not more than a few minutes she was telling me the problems she was experiencing within her relationship. She never gave any thought to the possibility that I might share the news with half the Gatineau Hills. Highandry's problems stem from the fact that her boyfriend seems to be turning towards homosexuality. "I'm a beautiful and hot blond, Tercel. I just don't understand why he's losing interest. He'd rather log onto the bi-sexual and homosexual chat rooms than get it on with me." My first impulse, of course, was to take advantage of the situation, do a little gay bashing and then give her my email address. But, unfortunately, the years I spent in an obviously misguided attempt at spiritual development have taken their toll. No longer capable of being a complete monkey, I found myself trying to convince her that it doesn't mean her boyfriend isn't still in love with her. I attempted to encourage her to free her mind a little, to become a bit more expanded in her thinking; that was my foolishness, I suppose. A very wise man I've known once told me that I'd do well to stop trying to change other people and concentrate on changing myself. Unfortunately, I've neglected his advice more than once or twice.

As the conversation progressed, however, I began to realize that Highandry was not a pleasant creature. No matter what I offered in way of soothing and kind words, she'd keep saying "This conversation's going nowhere," and "You guys just never understand girls like me," or even, "You're one of THEM aren't you?" In fact the lady became so abrasive by the end, though I'd tried to help all the while, that I signed off by writing, 'Madam, if I was your boyfriend I'd go gay also.' I know. I know. What a monkey.

26. Snakes

There's a charming, ancient saying in India that goes; 'Oh how I hate snakes! Kill it! Kill it! Kill the slimy creature! There's a boulder. Smash it!' Generally speaking, Indians are not overly fond of the reptiles. They worship them. They're fascinated by them. But they fear them as I do.

Nevertheless, the snake can be found again and again within the mythology of the Hindu religion. Lord Shiv, for example, wore a python as a necklace. And since a lovely lady, as the story goes, made it her business to interrupt his thousand years of meditation, one can only assume the snake didn't particularly turn her off. It may even have enhanced his rather rugged image, though it must also be pointed out that the relationship was a stormy one. Lord Krishna trounced a demon snake. Lord Vishnu used to sleep on one.

It took at least six months and several donations to the village temple before I was allowed to take away a large, stone carving I'd found embedded in a nearby hillside. Unfortunately, when it finally was dislodged, a thick, black snake wriggled around from behind it, sending the men, in a panic, galloping back to huddle under their cots for the rest of the afternoon. That left the tractor driver, who was too mentally challenged to even be superstitious, and myself, who was too ... oh well, to deal with the stone.

After a monumental effort, I succeeded in having the piece carted up to my house and built into one of my walls. I was very proud of it. The carving showed Lord Shiv, with bulging eyes and a snake around his throat, pouring clarified butter onto the rooftop of a temple that, strangely, was shown sticking up from between his legs. To the untrained eye, it would most certainly have looked weird, bizarre, even perverse. I lit candles in front of the carving and lay back on my bed to enjoy the thing in its glory. I couldn't. It was way too weird, bizarre and perverse for me.

I tried to imbibe its beauty and religious significance. But, after two days and three nights I hired the same men, who had carried it up, to take it back.

Indian sages liken death to a harmless rope that's mistaken for a dangerous, venomous snake in the dark of the night. When travellers realize their error, they're quite relieved. In the same way, they continue, when spiritual travellers realize the essential, eternal aspect of their self, they're obviously relieved forever.

And so, on one memorable occasion I returned to my Delhi hotel weighted down by far too many parcels to handle without precipitating hernias or hernia, whichever the case may be or might be. One of my more delightful acquisitions that day was a straw basket, such as any snake charmer would have. My basket, however, held within it a papier-mâché cobra instead of a real one, black with shimmering pieces of cut mirrors to look like scales. It had bright red zircon eyes and a bed of straw painted green. And when anyone lifted the lid, the snake would rise up slowly with the help of a spring. It was quite realistic. I thought it was very charming.

Two porters and I crowded the small, dimly lit elevator with all the packages, forcing a friendly and enthusiastic-looking Danish couple back into the corner. They must've been on their first trip to India with hopes of adventure and romance in the land of magic. They also must've had the usual dose of culture shock. Before the doors closed one of the porters, holding the snake basket on top of the others said, "Oh what a lovely basket sir." So I, wanting to be clever, suggested he lift the lid. When he did, the cobra raised its awful head; the porter let out a blood-curdling scream and threw the basket straight up. As he ran through the lobby he yelled, "Snake! Snake!" The other porter ran behind him as though they were in a qualifying event for the Asian games. The hapless Danish couple, trapped in the corner, yelled and wept and bounced from wall to wall while I lay on the ground laughing so hard I must've appeared to have been bitten. People were jumping over the front desk screaming and scattering out through the hotel doors.

When I last visited my brother's brand new house in a brand new subdivision of Toronto, I spotted a scrawny garter snake on their brand new lawn. My sister-in-law jumped a mile when she saw it, almost landing on top of me. And anyone knowing my sister-in-law knows that would've surely ruined my day. But, of course, once again I remembered India wistfully. Seeing that pathetic excuse for a snake, in that brand new tailor-made world, helped me realize that there may indeed be life on Mars. It also reminded me that it behoves us to keep in mind what's real and what's important. Because the rest will eventually slither away.

27. Let There Be Light

Writing this column by candlelight seems so very right. For when all's said and done, the message is that it's really one world, east or west. And whatever reminds me of that fact must be good. So, as I sit here inanely cursing Quebec Hydro, the government, the country, and even God, I remember how often I stewed in just this fashion whilst living in medieval India.

It's not that I believe these occasions, blackouts caused by severe storms, make me more enlightened or a better person. In fact, these occasions make me mad and hurt my eyes. They make the years I spent meditating and navel gazing, as I've heard it called somewhat patronisingly, seem questionable as I put a foot through my bedroom door. It's just that one can't help but remember at times like these that we weren't born with ovens and fridges, computers or televisions. Unfortunately, while I appreciate that point, as I'm sure my mother does, I've run out of matches and the wood's damned wet, my sprouts are wilting and the milk's going sour. What the hell am I going to do about dinner?

During my early years in India, villagers there would never have thought of depending on electricity. It would've been the height of foolishness. The houses were built with small rooms of thick stone and mud walls that a few candles could heat. On cold winter nights, whole families would snuggle up together or with small barnyard animals. And in those days my friends and I would huddle around our teacher, sometimes all through the nights, bake potatoes in the fireplace while listening to talks about the adventures of Vedic saints and sages. We'd sip hot Indian spice tea and read by candlelight until sleep would take us in waves to dream about forest kingdoms and experiences of a magical, mystical nature.

Later on, of course, the infrastructure improved, and we fell asleep dreaming of NYPD Blue, WWF Wrestling, NBA Basketball and CNN

News. Later on, of course, we ate lasagne cooked in ovens, drank coffee and sat in front of electric heaters. But, just when we'd become sure that the world was as it should be, and just when we most wanted our televisions, ovens and especially the heaters, a simple rainfall would wipe out our lines. Winter was still a cold, damp and foreboding time, a reminder that we are not in control there as we are not here. It would, however, become wonderfully quiet again, until people began to bring in the generators.

Some of the folks of my neighbourhood then began discussing what to do about those blasted generators. I still recall a meeting that lasted well over an hour, which I can assure you showed a greater attention span than was normal for that crew. We were trying to figure out a solution to the problems of one generator in particular, the one at the local gas station. It was needed, but it had a huge effect on the whole area, sitting on the roof of the office like a black dragon, bellowing and belching and declaring its supremacy over its kingdom. As usual, there was much flowery talk and even some great oratory. But, the discussion went round in circles with no agreement, although a simple brick building would've done the trick. Eventually, a local cobbler got to his feet and stated with authority that the problem was the generator at the gas station.

At that point in the proceedings, we adjourned the meeting with an idea to get together again another night. The electricity had come on again and everyone wanted to get back to watching the cricket game. India was beating Pakistan. So far as I know, except when one of the local boys poured sugar in its gas tank, that machine's still roaring. There are many differences as well as similarities between India and Canada. It's a theme that runs through these articles. For example, upon being invited to a friend's games room in New Delhi one would never expect to find a moose head mounted on the wall or a stuffed beaver in a ferocious pose on the floor. You'll see a snooker or Ping-Pong table. When you pick up your favourite shirt from the laundry over here, you don't expect to find holes in it from having been beaten to death during the cleaning process.

Both places have strengths and weaknesses. But, the lights have come back on now and I really have to watch 'Who Wants To Be A Millionaire.'

28. Beware of Sweet, Little Old Ladies

Once upon a time, deep inside our Himalayan Mountain ashram, Swamiji asked a visiting lawyer to explain what happens when a judge can't make a decision. The lawyer hemmed and hawed until Swami mercifully interrupted. "Nathan," he called out. "Your father's a judge. What would he do when he couldn't decide?" "That's easy," I said from the middle of the audience, "He'd just bring it up over dinner and mom would tell him what to do." The crowd went wild.

I sat in a courtroom last week for the first time since I was a wee little willy wanker watching dad loom large over the proceedings. Only this time I was the jerk on trial. On one of the first days living in Quebec, as I made my way from Ottawa to my day job in Alcove, and while driving through an intersection in Hull, a car broadsided me. When I got out of my poor, beaten Tercel with its broken wing, I was angry and upset. But, I quickly noticed that an old lady had been driving the other car. So I put my arm around her and asked if she was all right. I stroked her back, spoke to her soothingly and showed genuine concern. She looked up at me with a tear in the corner of one of her wise, kind old eyes and barked, "You bloody well went through a red light, you bastard!"

Needless to say, after the police arrived I hardly understood a word of whatever was said since I didn't speak French at the time. I still don't, but I thought it sounded better that way. Two men, brothers, offered themselves as witnesses to the fact that I went through a red light. I knew that because one of them broke from French long enough to turn and say in English, "Even if you didn't run the light, you were certainly pushing it and we like this little old lady better than we like you." And I was made to sit in my car for at least twenty minutes after everyone else was allowed to leave.

Having a mistaken understanding that Quebec has a 'no fault' insurance system, I went about getting my car fixed without bothering my insurance company. But, I really didn't feel good about pleading guilty to running a red light, so I just waited. In the meantime, my insurance company contacted me, having been contacted first by the old lady's insurers, and explained the facts of life and said they'd be doing an investigation. Much to my surprise, I received a letter a few weeks later stating that, not only did they believe my story, they realised it was the fault of the other party involved in the accident. They also pointed out that the witnesses recanted their testimony and would not appear in court. And they did not.

One full year later, sitting in court finally, I again could not understand a word of what was being said. Eventually, I was instructed in English to take a seat at the front while the sweet, little old lady was helped to the witness box. Everyone loved her instantly. But, I knew her better. They smiled when they looked at her. They frowned at me. No one wondered how a lady, so hobbled by arthritis that she had to use a walker, could be considered a driver beyond suspicion. No one asked how she could be so sure I'd gone through a red light. The lady pointed out that she had proceeded through a green light only to be shocked and dismayed when I smashed into her. No one pointed out that it was she who ran into the side of my car. After saying her piece, she walked slowly with her walker back to her seat while several people leaned forward to help.

By the time my turn came, I was terribly nervous. My head was throbbing. I'd never been in any situation like that in my life. I managed to point out the simple fact that I hadn't hit the lady, that she'd smashed into the side of my car. That was said to be irrelevant. It was irrelevant that I never hit anyone. Then I produced a letter from my insurance adjuster only to be told that it was inadmissible evidence. I was never allowed to say that the witnesses, their presence at the scene being the only reason I was charged in the first place, had changed their testimony. I was not allowed to say anything about that.

In short, it came down to the word of the sweet, little old lady against mine, an obviously hardened criminal type. I was dead in the water. The process of licking my wounds later included, of course, a call to my dad. After he listened carefully to my story, sympathetically, I asked his opinion and what he thought I might do. He said "Well, Nathan, I'm really not sure. Perhaps you should ask your mother."

29. The Immortals

On Thursday, July 8, 1999 an article appeared in the Ottawa Citizen that really shook my tree. It stated that, with the help of Fruit Flies, scientists have discovered the key to immortality. I rather like the idea of living forever but what ticks me off is the thought that kids of today may benefit from the breakthrough after I've already passed over to the other side. Imagining immortality being discovered after I die is a very irritating thought. Therefore, I'd like to fervently urge the government to facilitate further funding for Fruit Fly experimentation.

Up until now, my dealings with flies of any sort have not been particularly positive. We've had a troubled relationship. The British Columbia Horse Fly used to torture me while I planted trees back in the early seventies. Planters used to say that if you stopped moving for five minutes you'd get sick and if you stopped for ten you'd die. The Indian House Fly, of course, bugged me for years both in my home and at the local cafés where I'd have to eat with one hand while waving off hordes of them with the other. The Tse Tse Fly infected me with malaria, which gave me a few bad turns I can assure you.

Before ever going to India, I travelled to Hawaii in search of the quietest, most peaceful spot in the world to meditate. I was labouring under a mistaken belief that silence was paramount for good meditation. I decided to trek down into the dormant volcano, Haliyakalu, on the island of Maui. It was the work of a full day to reach the wooden cabin built at the bottom, obviously just for me. I felt I had finally found the best possible situation for deep, uninterrupted meditation, contemplation and prayer. You could hear a pin drop. There wasn't a sound, not a soul around. I rolled out my mat and, with a great sense of satisfaction, plopped myself down. I was in heaven.

Unfortunately, a noisy fly flew fairly frequently in. I never knew a fly could cause such a racket. Soon, several flies were dancing around the cabin as if they were at the El Mocombo on a Saturday night. There were no screens on the windows, so I was compelled to watch, and curse, them all night long. I left early the next morning. The good news is I've been able to do a creditable mime of a fly preening itself ever since, which has in fact come in handy at parties.

In any event, it may just perhaps be payback time and, while I admit to a certain scepticism, I also feel a certain grudging gratitude. It must be pointed out that the only ones to benefit so far from the experiments are the flies themselves, living up to three times their normal life-span while no doubt smugly watching the scientists shrivel around them. The scientists claim, as a matter of fact, that even when the flies die it is not due to old age. They're weakened by mechanical breakdown. Whatever. So is my Toyota. Either way you're still dead. More work obviously needs to be done, and the sooner they get to it the better.

I knew a homeopathic doctor in India who thought that one could become immortal by eating a slip of paper with a certain label of salts pencilled on it. He'd scribble on a scrap of paper, hold it to his forehead for a few moments before gobbling it down. And he's still alive as well as being fairly independent at nearly fifty years of age! Ginseng, wheat-grass, facelifts and babies are all, one way or another, attempts at a piece of immortality and I'm in favour of them all. My grandmother has a park named after her. It's north of Toronto, in case you get the urge to visit Vanek Park at Lake Wilcox.

Saint Seraphim of Sarov, a great Christian saint of the sixteenth century, used to carry a sack of boulders wherever he went in an attempt at eternal life in the spirit. Ramakrishna used to sit in full lotus posture with eyes closed for days on end with a belief that by doing so he'd experience the pure Aatma or eternal Self. I, myself, have made some humble efforts in that regard, and look how well adjusted I am.

We want most of all to remember ourselves not as one little wave with a beginning and an end, but as the whole vast ocean of life. And that's the point.

30. Sarah Brings You Down

Sarah was convinced that the more subtle the diet, the more ethereal, angelic and spiritual one would become. In the early seventies, she went from carnivore to vegetarian, fruitarian and then to what she called a breatharian. I never made it quite that far, although I respected her tremendously. To this day, whenever I go to a restaurant with my parents, dad announces my culinary peculiarities to all the patrons pretty much before seats are assigned. With an arm wrapped affectionately if not patronisingly across my shoulders he'll say in a booming voice, spoken as one who has been compelled to come to grips with a situation one can't ever really condone, "My son here is a vegetarian! What do you have in your restaurant for him?"

Although I used to be quite a fanatical vegetarian, I was never militant. And over the years I've mellowed. As a matter of fact, I'd like to share with my readers some news of a great invention to test how well cooked your meat is. I saw it advertised on television just the other night. It's called the Truecook Fork. You'll wanna be careful with the spelling. All you have to do is stick the Truecook Fork (try saying that three times quickly), in your steak, chicken, pig or fish and a thermostat tells you if the meat's rare, medium rare, well done or burned. Isn't that wonderful? Handy for family barbecues. I tried one out on my buddy's Labrador Retriever with marvellous results. She was quite rare at the time, but I understand that may change if she doesn't stop trying to hump the sofa.

On their recent visit to my place in Wakefield, their first time out here, my folks positively adored the Alpengruss Restaurant. They both agreed it was the best restaurant dinner they could remember having. And, while it is true they often don't even remember who I am, it's fair to assume they meant it. They were still talking about that meal as we gathered for tea at my place next morning. They'd decided to share one of those mammoth, tasty cinnamon rolls from the famous Wakefield Bakery. Were I to eat one myself, I'd be walking strangely for a week after.

As they climbed the steps to my house, I received a mini-lecture from dad about the poor condition of the cement stairs. He was quite right of course and we discussed it, along with other important issues, over tea. He ate most of the cinnamon roll, having fallen off his 'no wheat' diet wagon, while mom sipped tea stoically. On the way out, mom walked ahead while dad again noticed the broken stairs. "Well, you wouldn't have to fix them all" he allowed. "Don't tell me I didn't have to eat it all!" mom yelled back, "You ate it all!" They were still arguing the point as they drove away, no doubt never realising that they were talking of two totally different issues.

The better restaurants all over India, by and large, have two kitchens. One kitchen is for vegetarian and one's for non-vegetarian. The roadside cafes are often not quite so discerning, and peeking into their kitchens would not go a long way in stimulating one's gastric juices. I've looked down into my lentil soup and seen a well-cooked cockroach looking back up as if to say, 'I zigged when I should've zagged.' In my own home, I once found a mouse had gotten into the honey pot and slipped inexorably down, down, down to a bitter/sweet end. It put me right off my morning toast.

Not long after meeting Sarah, I did become a fruitarian whilst living in Mexico for over a year. I became a believer in the Arnold Aerhardt Mucousless Diet Healing System. It was quite a remarkable experience and I felt it was 'the true way.' Then one evening I read a newspaper article about how Doctor Aerhardt had died after being accidentally hit over the head with a lead pipe. I suppose I fell into some kind of existential funk then, trundled off to consume a chicken dinner, and was promptly stricken by 'Montezuma's Revenge.'

A few days later, some good people offered me a ride to San Francisco, but they got fed up with having to stop the car every few minutes for me to go off to the bushes. So one of them gave me a pill. That plugged me up pretty well, but my ankles began to look as if they belonged on an elephant. And that's the way they stayed until I waddled into the men's room at the Ramada Inn in Tucson, Arizona, and all hell broke loose. I went from stall to stall obliterating the plumbing; and I do believe they had to renovate after I got finished with the place.

Sometime in the mid-seventies I heard that Sarah had died. Nobody knew much about Anorexia or Bulimia back then. But, it did occur to me that we're just not meant to be that ethereal.

31. Prevention's Always The Best Medicine

On a damp, dark night last week I was driving down the Notch road when a deer darted out of the dense bush. That was darned near the death of me. I might've died from the collision or from sheer fright of it, but my stout heart survived yet again. I'm not sure how the deer felt about our near-death experience. He or she didn't stop to chat, though I was close enough to actually tell whether it was a he or a she. Unfortunately, one almost always forgets to check at those times. Hardly fifty feet ahead a sign came into view reminding all drivers to beware of deer crossing the road.

Would that one could always view the signs before the accidents. I'm sure the world would be a better place. If only we knew to avoid the pitfalls on the roads of our lives we'd be laughing. Would that I could've known my old friend had become a flake over the years; I may have thought twice about inviting her for a visit. I actually rather like flakes. Some of my best friends are flakes. But, Heather had also become ... a psychic! And psychics always see too darned much.

Unlike that ominous night on the Notch Road, the signs were there beforehand. I just didn't bother reading them. I couldn't know, however, that even part of her family left town when they heard she was coming. When the time came, I made the best of it, spent the night contentedly on my couch and in the morning asked how she'd slept. She complained bitterly about some folks being in bed with her and I was perhaps a little quick to point out that I hadn't been one of them, but that's not what she'd meant. Apparently, some 'entities' follow her around wherever she goes, which I felt was stretching my hospitality just a bit, really.

Being psychic would've come in handy as I went to meet a buddy for a swim in Chelsea earlier this very week. Following a hot time in the city, I arrived down at the river there only to find the whole area lousy with sport utility vehicles. So I wheeled my trusty little Tercel back up the severe, rutted, dirt road to level ground and looked for a reasonable parking spot. I chose a place in nobody's way and yet, as I began to lock up, a guy yelled from a second floor window of a house way back from the road that I was not welcome to park in front of his manicured lawn.

Would that I could've known that particular house, with its manicured lawn and trimmed bushes, was owned by a fellow who obviously needs more roughage in his diet. I'd have simply been able to choose another before being scolded. Unfortunately, parking was at a premium there that day. He said it'd be different if he knew me, so I yelled "How do you do? I'm Nathan. Now can I park here?" But, he was having none of it, and I was a little sorry I had used my real name.

Had Doug foreseen that I didn't know fuel from gas, dix from that, up from down, he may have thought twice about hiring me. (Of course he still would've.) But, long after leaving my job at Ryan's Famous Garage and Towing Company, and while still missing the place, whenever I wheel in for a fill-up I'm tempted to spread some of the stuff around under that car just for old-times sake. I'm tempted to miscalculate my own change, speak Hindi when I should speak French to whoever's around, ask Super Dave what 10W30 means, what gas-line antifreeze is, how to change a wiper, replace a headlight . . .

Would that we had known pesticides cause breast cancer. We could've banned them much earlier, and our mothers, sisters and aunts might still be alive. Would that I had known in 1975 that I'd not return until the very end of the millennium. I might not have gone to India. (Of course I still would've.) In fact, I can't say I wasn't warned. At the conclusion of my first meeting with my teacher, as I walked away towards the room he had arranged for me, I heard him call out "You'd better think carefully about staying, Mr Nathan. Because if you stay ten days, your whole life's going to change."

Would that we could know what awaits us upon the dissolution of these bodies, these mortal coils as it were. We'd be better prepared. There's a wise old saying in India that goes, 'always keep the thought of death in one hand and God in the other.'

32. Sometimes Life Rubs Me Wrong

In 23 years of living in India I never had fleas the likes of which I experienced recently right here in Wakefield. Or so I thought. Not being able to sleep, itching like a son of a gun, I finally decided to take a bath. Normally, I don't like taking baths at my place; nor do I like guests taking baths at my place. Because it seems that one or two baths and I have to get the holding tank pumped. However, the bath helped, somewhat, and in the early morning light I even got a few minutes shut-eye.

Unfortunately, I awoke itching worse than ever. Grandma used to say you should never scratch. You should rub. And rub I did because I always listened to grandma's sage advice. The rubbing advice was right up there with how best to make French Fries. That's why I couldn't understand why my whole body began to look like I'd been last man out of the jungles of Vietnam.

It quickly became obvious I needed to do something drastic. So I purchased the very best bug spray that borrowed money could buy, and I blasted my place. I zapped every inch of every pillow, blanket, carpet and especially the mattresses. I shut the place up tighter than a drum and went to town for a cappuccino. Upon my return, over lunch at the ever-popular Chez Eric's restaurant, a friend took one look at my fleabites and announced it wasn't fleas at all. It was poison ivy! I soon found myself dining alone in the garden, everyone having opted instead and all of a sudden to luncheon at the Earl House.

The occasion reminded me of a leper I saw once in a town near where I lived. He was a tall good looking sort, as lepers go, who just unfortunately had no hands, no nose to speak of, barely any toes and carried his tin can around with its handle draped across his arm. He'd approach tourists looking somewhat pathetic, swaths of cloth over his stumps, unkempt and sad eyes, hoping for a rupee or three. More often than not, the people would take one look at him and scurry off into a shop or alleyway. On a misty Himalayan morning I spotted the leper approaching a tall lady in the market with tin can outstretched. The lady was taken by surprise, repelled and turned away. He persisted, which caused the lady to move deeper into the market. As I watched, however, she seemed to have a change of heart, returned and plunked a couple of coins into the leper's can before rejoining her group.

The leper followed the lady. He tapped her on the shoulder with his stump, which I have no doubt she remembered that night in her dreams. He asked somehow for one of her cigarettes. Having decided to connect with the poor creature at all, I suppose the lady figured she might as well go all out and acquiesce to his request. Placing a cigarette in the leper's can, she turned away, which I found odd since he couldn't very well light it himself. He must've also thought it odd because he followed behind, again, and tapped her shoulder, again, motioning for some further assistance.

The lady obviously had had quite enough interaction with the leper to satisfy her need to be magnanimous, so she gave him her Bic lighter in rather perfunctory fashion. The leper had no clue what it was, held it between his two stumps and looked curiously at the liquid through its opaque casing. Of course he had no fingers to manipulate the thing, even if he could've figured it out. So he followed after the tall lady and once again tapped her on the shoulder. By that time one could almost believe the two were on a first name basis. At least the lady must've regretted ever having decided to be, of all things, open-minded. And while she may have silently decided to never ever make the same mistake again, to her credit she took that lighter and lit his fag with a smile and placed another, along with the lighter, into his tin can. It certainly made his day, and mine. I should also add, however, that the woman insisted her group move along pronto after that, without looking back.

With that fond memory still flickering through my mind, I picked up my satchel and my tin can and left Chez Eric's. That night, however, as I lay down to sleep, mashing my face into the pillows and rubbing my legs incessantly, I couldn't help feeling fairly frustrated. For, although it turned out I didn't have fleas, it turned out I still had to ingest the effects of the flea spray. And I thought, 'what an unfamiliar world this still is.'

33. Northern Dancer

It seemed that every time I tuned in to the Pan American Games, held recently in Winnipeg, some high-jumper, volley-baller, swimmer or roller-hockeyer had been caught taking banned substances. It seems obvious that most athletes do take performance-enhancing drugs. It seems further that it's just a matter of who's unlucky enough to be tested, who misjudged the time needed for the stuff to clear through their system, who was so shit-faced they just plain forgot.

I'm willing to entertain the possibility that I'm being too cynical. I saw an interview with a track star categorically denying ever having taken drugs to help his hurdling. Unfortunately, he was a shot-putter. And I still would've taken him at face value except he kept pawing at the ground. His agent placed a sugar cube in his mouth and rubbed his nose at the end. There was actually a hurdler caught with so much stuff in his system he was odds-on favourite to win this year's Grand National Steeplechase.

I would like to vehemently deny rumours that I've ever taken performance-enhancing drugs. I have taken drugs that rendered my performance rather pathetic, but that's another story. When I was eighteen, one night I returned home, tripping on LSD, to find my mother in the kitchen waiting up for me. She looked concerned, but for the life of me I couldn't figure out who she was. I wasn't even entirely sure what species I was dealing with. So when she said my father, the judge, found some things in my room he wanted to ask me about in the morning, it didn't really mean much to me. I prostrated to what I thought was a photo of the queen, but which I later discovered was the fireplace, wished all beings peace and love, then floated off to bed. Somehow, I found the way to my room and lay down.

Sleep was not something I expected that night. Instead, I watched the many winged fairy people fluttering around, blowing me kisses and trying on my clothes. Mostly the clothes were too large, which made them look silly. In the morning, as I went up to the kitchen, the judge was waiting. I recognised him right away, put my arms against the wall and spread my legs. In fact, I hadn't remembered my mom's warning at all until that moment. But, when dad said he wanted to discuss something he found in my room, I got defensive. "Dad," I jumped in with both feet. "I've been thinking about it all night," I lied, "and don't see why I should be ashamed. So what if you found my stash. So what if I smoke dope! You drink alcohol and I smoke dope. So what?!" While defending my position, employing grandiose hand gestures for emphasis, I noticed my mother's jaw drop. I noticed the look of horror spreading across the judge's face, but I still didn't realize I'd made a slight blunder. Slowly, however, the fog cleared. I soon realised that dad had merely found some matches, a few butts and wanted me to fess up to smoking cigarettes.

Some people leave home when its time to go to college. Some people strike out on their own to get married or live with their girlfriend or boyfriend or any number of mixes and matches. I left home after admitting, for no good reason whatsoever, that I do smoke, and inhale, marijuana. Not that my parents wanted me to leave. It's just that the scene that ensued, with my dad's threats of rehab and/or counselling and my mom's wailing and gnashing of teeth, was such a bummer that I really felt my time there had come to an end.

Several years later, during the very first meeting I ever had with my guru, he pointed out that to be a yogi meant giving up all intoxicants of any sort, including even cigarettes. In fact, I had already stopped everything earlier, which, depending on your point of view, was a shame when you consider how much stuff grows wild all around that area of India. Right below where I was living, there were fields of marijuana so high a person could get lost in there for days. And many did. On several occasions I'd find a wandering mendicant standing in the midst of the plants with a silly smile, rubbing the leafs methodically, even religiously, to make hashish for their pipes. They'd often ask if I've noticed any of the winged fairy people fluttering around.

Those athletes caught with their hands in the cookie jar, so to speak, will have to live with a sense of shame, right or wrong. Ben Johnson was disgraced even though he could run like Northern Dancer. And I, well, you guessed it. I'm high on life.

34. Sacred Path
Card Readings

Annette Sabela gazed meaningfully at the card I had chosen from her deck. It was called "Smoke Signals." Reading from her book and with a minimum of personal interpretation, she explained that I really need to figure out what the purpose of my life is. I was rather hoping she would just tell me, but apparently that's not how it works.

Pointing out that it's of utmost importance to recognise the power of our own understanding, Annette stressed the cards are "designed to allow that personal talent be used." In a refreshingly straightforward sort of way, while her five-month-old Eric's laughter reached us from the porch, Annette added that the Sacred Path readings could be used as a toy or for deeper understanding. Personally, I think it's hard to beat a good rattle, but then I'm the one who needs to figure out what the purpose of my life is.

The author of the book as well as the cards was an American lady by the name of Jamie Sams who studied with the Seneca, Lacota, Iroquois and Apache wisemen, went on vision quests and eventually asked the elders for permission to share the ancient knowledge. I couldn't quite ascertain whether Sams was actually Indian. In her book, however, Sams writes that "The purpose in reopening these lesson paths for others is to promote understanding, peace between all creeds, all nations, all clans, all tribes and families." In order to help recreate the 'uniworld' we come from, she devised a 'system of divination,' to help all 'two-legged' ones remember we're one being, one life.

Once in a while I come across a philosophy, an understanding that rings true and pure. With its talk of the silence of a seeking heart, the Sacred Path feels like one such philosophy or understanding. And with her talk of wanting to know why we're on this planet, and wanting to help, Annette's sincerity and total absence of pretension is a pleasure to behold. But, I'm not sure what the 'elders' would think of a lady as white as my ... house carrying on the tradition of the 'Sacred Path.'

Like Jamie Sams, 38-year-old Annette waited a long time before she felt prepared to share her knowledge with the rest of us two-legged ones. Having fallen in love with the Wakefield area, and moving here from Ottawa in 1988, Annette lived on Burnside Avenue, worked at the Black Sheep Inn, and even at The News for a short while. For the past ten years, however she's worked in the dental clinic of the Children's Hospital in Ottawa, from which she's presently on maternity leave.

Annette's husband, ("in the eyes of God,") is 42-year-old Mr Richard Charles Penderell Prodger, formerly of Great Britain, in case the reader was in any doubt, and is now a finishing carpenter in the area. And nine-year-old Sebastian, from a former marriage, completes the picture.

On the afternoon of my visit, rain was threatening. Annette often views even thunder and lightening as messages from allies in the spirit world. And if that's really the case, I rather wish the allies would leave my electricity alone. "The gift of wisdom," she says in her understated way, "is in the heart of the recipient." Apparently, it's important to think of any question one wants answered while shuffling the cards. Annette then takes the deck and fans them out. You can choose one card, but you can also opt for a more in-depth session by choosing seven. And, while it's not a business, Annette accepts donations, barters or smiles, and good wishes. I'm not sure if she'd accept automobiles or microwaves. I know I will. You'd best ask her at: (819) 827 3364.

I've never been much inclined towards Tarot Cards, Tao Te Ching or Gin Rummy, either for that matter. I've been known to get downright cranky when coerced into a Reiki treatment. I'm not inclined to invest in Noni juice, crystals or Tibetan Singing Bowls. And I won't be running to Annette whenever I'm experiencing an epiphany in my life. But, I'm also capable of feeling quite humbled in the face of such simple honesty, sincerity and a desire to do good the likes of which I found slightly hidden on the Notch road this past week.

35. *This Is Not Kansas*

Starting a new job's often a traumatic experience. Certainly, most people don't make a mess in their pants en route to the first day, but even though I once worked with the same company, it was nearly two decades ago. Also, although I did have my own shop in India for twelve years, it was so very different. My business was one of the most sophisticated in the Himalayas, but that doesn't mean a whole lot. Although it was a thriving little business, it was carried on mostly under the table. And I can assure you it used to get pretty darned crowded under there.

Howard's Jewellers on Sparks Street has now hired two 'sales consultants' at the same time; my good self, as we say in India, and a squat little woman from Lebanon who, in 1977, was one of the hostages held at the Canadian embassy in Beirut. Not noticing any similarity between her experiences as a hostage all those many years ago and the situation in which she now finds herself, Ramona's heartfelt ambition is to climb up the corporate ladder to the rung labelled, 'manager.' My own personal ambition is somewhat more modest. I'd just like to learn to use the telephone properly.

On the second day, Ramona and I were instructed in how best to answer the phone. After our lesson the manager suggested Ramona first demonstrate her new knowledge. "Good morning. Howard Jewellers. Ramona speaking. How may I help you?" The manager was very pleased. "That's exactly how to answer the phone," she said in way of congratulations. Ramona beamed with pride. One biscuit was placed in her mouth. "You try now, Nathan. Try to do it the same as Ramona did."

"Good morning," I began. "Howard's Jewellers. Ramona speaking. How may I help you?"

For the next hour I practised proper style until, with everyone else busy, the phone rang. It rang several times. I gingerly picked up the receiver. I was nervous, full of trepidation, afraid my pants might become full of something other than trepidation. "Good afternoon," I began. "Howard Jewellers. Nathan calling. How may I help you?" A couple of days later, in the middle of another busy time, I answered the phone, "Ryan's Garage and Towing."

The first client I actually served was a guy who had lost his very valuable wristwatch while water skiing. I showed the fellow a watch, the same exact type he'd lost. After putting it on, he had trouble figuring out how to take it off again and asked me how. "Oh, we usually recommend water skiing," I said. With my peripheral vision, honed through years of mediocre basketball, I could see my employer shaking his head sadly.

Later the same day a few of my colleagues and I were discussing the state of the world together when a real man, all suited and booted up, approached. He wanted to hand in his Rolex watch for refurbishing, which I assumed meant an oil change, tune-up and stuff like that. He went on and on ad nauseam about how long he's had the watch and, after handing it over, how naked he felt without it on. "I just feel naked without it. You know what I mean?" he said looking to me for understanding. "Oh sure," I commiserated. "I feel like that every time I take my clothes off." My employer just kind of stared at me.

Having said all that, I should add that I'm really feeling positive about the job, that I really like the folks. Still, at the end of the day, when I take those expensive dress shoes off, put on my b-ball shoes and walk down past The Byward Market to my car, I feel like I'm floating. Then, when I drive out along the highway, as the sky puts on its colour show just for my drive back, I feel quite fortunate. And when I turn down into oh so charming Wakefield Village, to the river, wave to someone I know, wave to another I don't know, I feel blessed. It's good to get home.

36. Business Notes

In the shop where I work, it's very important never to forget to lock the jewellery cabinets. Due to the fact that I tend to forget what I'm doing after about every two minutes, that's a big problem for me. Observing the elegant sophistication with which the company is run, I look back on my own former business in India with a strange mix of dread and longing. There's so much I can learn from my present situation. But, there's a lot that my employer could learn from my past experiences as well. I don't know what those lessons would be, but it sounded good that way.

Certainly, I feel safe in saying that my little business in India was more holistic. I had no set hours, no book-keeping to speak of and virtually no one was in charge. Of course, there wasn't much money either, but I don't believe that should necessarily be the purpose of running a business. Nobody's going to convince me that getting all suited up and scraping your face with an intensely sharp, lethal instrument each morning before six or seven is natural. Nobody's going to convince me that being incarcerated in an excessively well-illuminated shop each morning before nine is natural. Have you ever seen even one of the pigeons on Sparks Street at that time of day? No. They have the good sense to start only after about ten thirty. I know. I've been watching. One or two may be seen as early as eight, but those are the birds on the fringes of pigeon society, the aberrations, the oddballs.

Also, I'm fairly convinced that if I work in that climate-controlled building for more than a year or so I'll suffer from oxygen deprivation. And while some may think I need not concern myself overly with the possibility of brain damage, I'd like to at least maintain my current level of intellectual capability. As well, one has to consider the very real possibility of a miscarriage in case of a blessed event in my life.

In the early days of trying to carve out a living in India from the rocks, literally, I used to travel around with a satchel full of money and jewellery, both mine and others, on my business trips. I didn't really know any better. Needless to say, a large portion of my net worth would be in that bag and one day it went missing. The only place I could remember having it last was in a scooter rickshaw. Unfortunately, there were upwards of ten thousand scooter rickshaw in Old Delhi and, like certain ethnic groups, they all looked pretty much the same to me. Nevertheless, I walked the streets of Chandni Chowk, the gold market, the silver market, the Red Fort and even the textile market hoping beyond hope to retrieve my bag, my very life.

All my years of meditation up to that point went for naught as a panic slowly built up in the pit of my stomach. And for once I couldn't blame it on amoebas. The chances of finding my bag intact faded with each street and alley I shuffled down. Whatever rickshaw wallah who had found the satchel, of course, would've purchased a piece of land in the Kangra Valley by then, a hovel, a cow and arranged dowry for his eldest daughter. Still, I had no choice but to continue wandering, looking and hoping.

Eventually, it occurred to me that I had stopped at the Thomas Cooke office for a few minutes and, although I was pretty sure I'd seen the bag since then, I went to check anyway. As I entered, I noticed a huge crowd of people all standing around in a semi-circle. At first I thought there must be someone with a monkey doing backflips for a few rupees the likes of which one can see all over India. Either that or someone had a heart attack. But as I slipped through the crowd I saw everyone was staring down at my bag, waiting for the bomb squad. For a moment or two I just stood there letting a profound sense of relief wash over me. Then I grabbed the thing and headed for the door while the crowd grasped collectively in horror. I wondered at the spectacle of hundreds of people crowding in as close as possible to stare blankly down at a package they believed was a bomb. Had it been a bomb it would've blown them to smithereens at any moment, though I perhaps was not in a position to be too patronising just then. But, I had my bag.

My mom used to say I'd lose my head if it weren't attached to my shoulders. She could not know doctors would be able to perform head transplants by the end of the century. I read that bit of news the other day in the Citizen. In the meantime, I still have to remember to lock the cabinets.

37. Kumbh Mela 1

On a balmy afternoon last week I went to the Psychics and Seers Fair at the Nepean Sports Centre. They all knew I was coming, of course, but I was a little taken aback to see how small it was. There were hardly thirty or forty stalls and little shops set up in one of the large, airless rooms there. Many if not all the supernormal sciences were nevertheless represented.

There were people who professed to be clairvoyant, clairaudient and even clairsentient. Clairsentient, I understand, is when the practitioner receives strong feelings about his client and proceeds to advise him or her accordingly. I've had a few relationships like that. So I carried on to where there were tarot card readers, aura readers, mediums and larges. I met a young lady who could hold an object and receive vibrations of its owner. That would help her advise the client. I would've liked to get a reading from her, but the only article I could think to give her to hold was my wallet and I already knew what that would've told her. I couldn't very well rationalise paying thirty dollars to hear that my finances are in shambles.

For some reason watching a man, red-faced, eyes closed, rocking back and forth while holding the tiny hand of a wide-eyed girl sitting across the table, reminded me of the first time I left my teacher. In February of 1976 I wanted to join a six-month silent Vipassana Buddhist meditation retreat near Bombay. Before hopping on the bus I asked Swamiji for any last minute advice and he said, "Yes, Mr Nathan. My advice is: don't be a Buddhist. Be the Buddha." And with those words ringing in my ears I set off.

My first stop was in Ahallabad. Fifteen and a half million people, mostly Hindu pilgrims, collected at the banks of the Ganges River there on the occasion of the Kumbh Mela, which happens only once every twelve years. Although I wasn't feeling at all well, I walked through the grounds for miles taking it all in. The Naga Babas, naked with matted hair, crouched beside the holy river to make dead sure they'd be the first to bathe in the holy river each day. I saw a fellow who'd been buried up to his neck for nine days. He said hello in English as I passed. I saw a Baba with one totally withered arm since he'd held it aloft for many years. I saw the people, the animals, the life. And it occurred to me that I'd probably never see a spectacle to match the Kumbh Mela again in this life.

Eventually, sick and exhausted, I dropped down in the middle of a muddy path and proceeded to leave the waking state far behind. If I slept it was not a form of slumber I've ever had before. And when I regained consciousness I found myself in the centre of a circle of yogis chanting mantras near a fire that lit up the night. As I drifted off again I wondered how I'd gotten to that campsite, and for some reason I thought of the friends I'd left behind in the mountains.

A dim morning sun greeted me back to the world. The mist created a surreal and otherworldly effect. Someone had placed a bowl of curd and sweets in front of me that tasted amazing. I felt great, totally different from the day before. A large, lumbering man, walking with a distinct limp, came up, sat down cross-legged and began to tell me a fantastic, though all too familiar story with no introductions whatsoever. He told me of a man called Ram Chandre, a wrestler from Varanasi, whose sister had been brutally burned to death by her husband's family over a dowry dispute. He described the girl as having the blackest hair and the whitest, purest heart like Himalayan snow. Ram Chandre had avenged her death, but not without paying a terrible price. He had to run away, to leave his home, his friends, never to see his aged parents again. Before I could even ask why he'd shared that story with me, he asked if I'd visit his parents and tell them he was well.

It did seem odd that Ram Chandre would assume I was heading to Varanasi, though I was. But, as that thought flitted through my mind he smiled and said he knew also I was going to Bodh Gaya, Igatpurri near Bombay, but that I'd return to the wise man in the mountains eventually. Nothing surprised me by then, I agreed to his request and I'll tell you what happened next week.

38. Kumbh Mela 2

If you're at all like me, you will have long forgotten that I was going to narrate the end of a story this week. Normally, I have a window of opportunity of about five minutes to remember important details like that. Luckily, I made a note of it in my computer. If you're at all like me, you will have forgotten how I had written of my time at the Kumbh Mela in Ahallabad with fifteen million pilgrims and how one Mr Ram Chandre told me of the sad demise of his sister. You will have forgotten that I wrote how he'd escaped from Varanasi after avenging her murder and how he'd requested I visit his parents to say that he's doing well.

As I wandered away from Ram Chandre's camp though the Mela, through the multitude of devotees, a western girl and boy came running towards me in a state of near panic. With their packs on their backs they looked tired and disoriented. The boy grabbed my arm tightly and asked if I spoke English. When I said I did he quickly pleaded with me to direct them to the latrines. I could feel their pain. Trying to be helpful, I pointed to two parallel ropes stretching for miles. "Anywhere between those two ropes," I answered. They both looked horrified as they faded back into the crowd around them.

As a celebration of the long tradition of Yogic life in India, several gurus would take turns parading through the Mela, with their disciples, each day with varying degrees of pomp and lavishness. One such procession struck me as rather too grand, however, too ostentatious. The guru rode on top of a massive elephant colourfully decorated with ornamental red and orange Rajasthani-style carpets and matching headdress.

The guru, himself a big man with a thick black beard, wore saffron robes and several rudraaksh bead maalaas around his neck. Behind him many smaller, decorated elephants followed carrying his disciples. Hundreds of people flocked around the front elephant trying to touch its feet or tail in the belief that by just touching the mount of that guru all their desires or their hopes of enlightenment would be fulfilled. The Mahout, or driver, was clearly frightened. The beast side-stepped and twisted almost beyond control, but the great man just laughed and wagged his finger down at the people, unconcerned for his or their safety, revelling in his own glory. The crowd was in a frenzy, the elephant dangerously on edge.

In spite of myself I couldn't help trotting along beside the massive, skittish beast, caught up in the excitement of the moment, not even knowing who the man was, though quite sure I didn't like him for setting himself so far above everyone else. What about the idea that we're from one source, one life force? Quite suddenly the great man turned around on his howda and looked straight down at me for a few moments. I was frozen in his gaze as he seemed to speak to me through his eyes. "Yes, you're right," those eyes called down to me, "Only tell these people, not me." I stopped dead in my tracks as he rode off through the Mela. Someone yelled at me in Hindi while passing that I'd just been blessed by the universally famous Babaji, whom I had never heard of.

Since I had had just about enough of the Kumbh Mela by then, I left for Varanasi. I found the small, wooden house of Ram Chandre's parents after no small effort. Once inside, I saw photos of Ram Chandre as a student, a wrestler, and standing with an arm around his ill-fated sister. After being welcomed warmly by the aged couple and served hot chai, I relayed my message. I supposed my Hindi was not good enough because they called for the help of a neighbour who had thick glasses that made him look like an owl, but who spoke very good English.

The old couple seemed to become cranky and even a little angry as I relayed my message again, that time in English. In fact, they left the room with just one backwards glance by Ram Chandre's mother. I asked if I'd offended them in some way. The neighbour was looking at me as though he had just been startled. "We don't know why you are saying these things," he said. "Ram Chandre had been shot and killed by the police years ago as he tried to make his escape from this very house. He was shot right in front of his parents."

39. It Is Impolite To Point

I was having a hard time finding a doctor. Having looked high and low, I finally spotted one on Bank Street leaving a Hava Java café. I didn't wanna hava java, but I knew it was a doctor because he had a BMW. Although I'm not enthusiastic about being examined too closely, and I'm certainly not eager to be violated, everyone keeps harping on the idea that guys my age ought to be checked for prostate problems. What if he finds a problem? Or, worse, what if I like the procedure. And, even worse, what if I like the procedure AND I have a problem? That would make two problems. We may never know, however, since I can't get an appointment anyway.

Having followed the doctor along Bank Street to his clinic, I paid some money for a consultation with some vague hope of being reimbursed by the Quebec Hospital Insurance Program later on. I introduced myself to the doctor in short and he said straight away that, although I do obviously have a problem, although I'm obviously not normal, he couldn't do any tests without charging me one-hundred and fifty thousand dollars and the deed to my home. It turned out that what I really paid for was a twenty-minute tirade against the Federal Government of Quebec. Being quite fond of Quebec myself, I felt somewhat unwell by the time I was finally dismissed. I would've preferred that if he wasn't prepared to stick his finger ... that he at least not screw me.

I've since been told that some doctors in Ottawa will accept the Quebec insurance card which brings into question the criticism levied against Quebec by that doctor. It seems to me that if one wanted to slander the government over here one could bring up far better issues for the purpose, such as the ever-popular language police. I've heard the word 'fascist' used to describe that particular bit of legislation, though I would never utter it myself. I just heard it used is all. Personally, I don't have strong feelings either way about Quebec's sovereignty, though I resist change as a general rule of thumb. I do understand both sides. I would merely hope that I could continue to live in the beautiful land in spite of not speaking French, that no one puts me in a camp with electric fences and that I can get a doctor's appointment when I need one.

The next problem, of course, is that no doctor around here is accepting 'new patients.' One of the doctors at the Centre de Medicine de Wakefield was recommended by a friend eager to see me get you know whatted. So, I phoned and was told the clinic's not accepting any new patients. I said that I certainly could be considered an old patient, that I'm not getting any younger and also that I live right around the corner. She remained, however, adamant. I tried to reason with the lady by pointing out that if I don't get to see a decent doctor soon I might never become an old patient of anyone.

The receptionist referred me to a clinic in Hull, but I couldn't help wondering why that clinic accepts new patients. Perhaps the doctors there are so bad no one wants to go there. I have no intention of being poked by a lousy doctor. I want a good one, or at least a cute one. I figure it's the good clinics that don't accept new patients. It's simple logic, really, isn't it? She cheerfully told me the clinic she was referring me to is off the very first exit into Hull. I felt compelled to point out that, if I end up having to go all the way to Hull, I really wouldn't give a rat's tail if it's off the first or fourth exit and that was pretty much the end of that conversation.

In the end, I've decided to go see an acupuncturist for fifteen dollars. I've decided to start small, as it were. Since I could hardly understand the Vietnamese receptionist over the phone, she passed me over to someone who spoke English a little better, who I soon discovered was actually one of the patients. I concluded that any clinic where the patients take the appointments is my kind of place. So I get to visit a doctor after all, and I also get to keep my virginity. I can sleep in peace again.

40. Whisperings

One has always to keep in ones mind the possibility, nay the certainty that in every endeavour will come setbacks. Even as I took up the challenge of my current position in the jewellery shop, I was aware I'd stumble eventually, make a mistake, faux pas, boo-boo. I figured I'd leave a cabinet open, drop a ruby necklace and unwittingly tread on it. I figured I'd leave out a zero on a Visa transaction, lose a diamond on the carpet. So it was with no small feeling of incredulity that, when it finally came, the crime was my neglecting to lower the toilet seat.

Without me ever realising it, a person even higher up the corporate ladder than I, a normally even-handed and well-adjusted lady, had been reduced to a simmering percolator of resentment towards whichever man kept forgetting the simple courtesy of lowering the seat after urinating. And as soon as she discovered who it was, the boorish lout unfortunately being me, a torrent of semi-scalding scorn was hurled in my general direction. She could not know that, in spite of my expensive suits, shoes and accessories, having lived most of my adult life in a 'different' sort of third-world kind of place, she's lucky I aim for the bowl at all and not simply spray any old wall handy at the time. But, I dared not say so. I also dared not suggest she actually look to see if the seat is up or down. I certainly dared not ask why it was up to the males of the species to make sure the toilet seat is always in the right position to accept the supple derriere of the females among us or amongst us, as the case may be. I dared not say any of those things for, you see, she had fallen into the toilet and apparently not for the first time.

There came, as well, an idea to suggest that the men lurking about could lower the seat after using the toilet if the ladies would raise the seat up after they used it. The wear and tear on said seat would certainly be prohibitive and, anyway, I dared not say it. In truth, I understood her side of why, if the seat had to be in one position or other as a rule, it should be left down. Still, I couldn't help wondering if any of the numerous security cameras around the place had been trained perchance on the toilet in question at the precise moment that she'd fallen in. It's not something I'm particularly proud of, but I just couldn't help thinking that particular video would be a tremendous addition to this year's Christmas party. Of course, it was just a passing thought that I dared not say. Also, of course, the corollary to that passing thought was that of course I also thought it odd imagining such a possibility while being chewed out, but that's just me.

Having survived the first real test of my new life on Sparks Street, such as it is, I floated down past the Byward Market to my Tercel and contentedly chugged back to Wakefield. And as I sat in the yard, Gatineau trees began to whisper. What a strange day. They may have been trying to talk to me for some days, only it was that Thursday I listened. 'We're turning,' they kept saying. 'Don't expect us to remain the same. We're turning. But, we'll put on a final display for you.' I heard something about not wishing to be compared to last year or next. And I felt a hitherto unexplored part of my personality appreciate the trees, from the very sap coursing through their fibrous veins to the leaves spiralling down orange around my feet, as if for the first time. A neighbour's puppy lifted a hind leg against one, confident in the knowledge that no self-respecting tree would ever mind.

Needless to say, in India trees don't whisper, or there aren't enough of them to hear. They aren't so confident or so sure of themselves. In India, the very lack of trees causes flash floods that wipe out whole villages, mudslides, and cold nights, due to the distinct scarcity of firewood. And so it happened that I concluded if the trees can deem me worthy of their attention, if they can exhibit that much unconditional love, I could not in all conscience remain stagnant. I had to do better.

41. Scissor Hands

Haircuts can be tricky. They can change the whole way you feel about the world. One day you're a stud-muffin, the next day you're walking around feeling like Tiny Tim tiptoeing through the tulips. And on this side of the great pond I've noticed they're also rather pricey. One seems to have a choice over here. You can meet your mortgage payment or get a decent hair cut. In India you can spend as much as you like, but you'll still come out looking like a freak of nature. Your hair will be marine short on the sides, move up and out to the little mop the barber leaves on top no matter in how many languages you've asked him to make it even all around. However, at least over there it costs very little to look silly.

Barbers in India can be found with a chair and mirror on roadsides or in fancy five-star hotels. Needless to say, they're almost all called The Gandhi Hair Cutters, Gandhi Barbers or Gandhi Stylists. Actually, they're usually called The Gandhi Har Cruttes, Gandhi Babres or Gandhi Stylits. One comes out looking the same whether from the Hyatt Regency Hotel or from a chair set up next to a ditch. As a matter of fact, the fellow on the side of the road usually gives quite a remarkable two-minute head massage after poodling you as well. No extra charge. It'll leave you disoriented and addled, but it's an inexpensive and legal way to experience an altered state of consciousness without too many side effects.

I would also like to warn any clean-cut would-be Indian travellers to never go to the same shop more than twice for a shave. The first time one visits a barber there, attracted by the incredibly low cost of a professional shave, he's proud and inspired to have a white-faced, sensitive-skinned foreigner sitting in his chair. He'll be very careful, use a new blade, hot water and shave with flourish and skill. The second time can go either way. The third time, however, you're asking for trouble. The barber takes you for granted by then. He'll have reverted back to his usual style of using the same old, dull blade he's used for the past several days to save money. He'll shave you while watching a cow grabbing carrots from the vegetable stall across the road. He'll talk to his friends, wipe the razor on a sleeve, clear his nose onto the street while still swiping away at your face.

Since I've been in Wakefield, a friend, formerly a professional stylist, has been kind enough to cut my hair. And she's very good. I've been spoiled. Unfortunately, I have a tendency to be rather impulsive. So, while at my day job on Sparks Street last week, nothing would do but that I have my hair cut during that very lunch hour. I asked someone I work with where I should go, and he directed me to a little shop around the corner. I should've known I was in trouble when I saw the candy-stripe sign out front. That means they charge next to nothing, which is what you usually get. There were three barbers. The first was old enough to be my ... elder brother, with long, wavy, grey hair, looked quite sour and cut hair without actually looking. The second was an Elvis impersonator, ducktail included and belly hanging down below his belt. I was sure I'd dropped a loony into the third one's hand that morning on the bridge as I trudged like a zombie to work. He looked as though he'd been through a few benders and sported a red, cherubic face and orange hair. He looked worse than me.

All three customers there at the time were having buzz cuts, so it's not as if I could tell if any of the barbers had some actual skill. I began to fear that it was the only style they did. The fellow who'd directed me there had a buzz cut as well. I drew the old guy and absolutely didn't understand one word he said as I sat squirming in the chair. It was all Greek to me. I later learned that he actually is Greek. Although I pleaded with him to cut my hair even all around, I came out of there with marine short sides moving up and out to the little mop left on top. I'm being made to feel at home in so many ways.

42. The Greatest Power There Is

Gurus, spiritual teachers, do tend to roam in predatory packs, herds or gaggles along the flat lands of the Indian Deccan. Now, large numbers have migrated to the new world and are stalking urban and rural centres even as I write this. This is, after all, the New Age.

In 1976 I was meditating in silence with my teacher of that time, U. S. N. Goenka, and with about two hundred other people from around the world for six straight months in Igatpurri, India. We were not supposed to utter a word, have eye contact, read, write or exercise other than a little stretching. We were, however, encouraged to keep breathing.

Near the end of the six months an American fellow, who had joined more recently, for some reason or other got it into his head that Goenka was a Jim Jones-type-of-guy, the anti-Christ, a demon, a devil.

I'd seen it all before. He was convinced we were all about to drink the poison cool-aid at teatime. I, on the other hand, had the advantage of actually knowing Goenka. He could be a trifle severe at times, but that was hardly reason enough to call in the FBI or the DEA. And I'd lived through innumerable tea times. There is strong evidence now, all these many years later, that the sugar was rotting our teeth. But otherwise the stuff was harmless. And if anyone had suggested leaving out the sugar I might've killed him or her myself. We're talking serious sense deprivation here, don't forget.

Only four days into his time there, the hapless fellow decided that Goenka was bad, broke the sacred vow of silence, and walked about the grounds crying out to try and save us. It must've been strange and discomforting, not to speak of eerie, pleading passionately to a bunch of silent, slow-moving people who wouldn't pay attention or even acknowledge him. I was in the bathroom brushing my teeth that morning when our American would-be saviour scurried in. The other people there at the time shuffled out as he ranted on about Goenka having taken over our minds. I continued to brush my teeth slowly, with concentration. I wasn't about to rush the one small pleasure I had before the day of sitting on my zafu began. Brushing one's teeth is not usually thought of as something one really waits for or looks forward to. After several months at that place, however, brushing one's teeth felt like an orgy of sensual delight. It was four-thirty a.m.

As disconcerting as it may have been to plead to a group of silent and slow-moving zombies who wouldn't pay any attention, I'm sure it was much worse trying to plead his case to me alone that morning. As he ranted on, I watched him through the mirror with a big, silly grin on my face. I just couldn't resist. I continued to brush my teeth in silence, nodding my head up and down in complete agreement, grinning, with Colgate dribbling down my chin. Eventually he stopped, looked hard at me, and ran out into the darkness.

Soon after, we were all meditating in the main hall. Goenka was sitting on his platform and, since I had been at the monastery longer than most, I was allowed to sit in the front row facing him. There were hardly three weeks left, and the vibration in the room, to say the least, was deeply peaceful. There was a ringing in the room, the sound of profound and utter stillness.

I hardly heard the American fellow running in yelling, "I have to save you! I have to save you! You don't see what he's doing to you!" I didn't even open my eyes. It seemed to be happening far away. I was unaware of him running up towards Goenka with a club until he reached the front; by then it was too late. I doubt I could've moved quickly enough anyway. I saw the boy yell and lift the club up high even while Goenka's eyes were still closed. But, just as the club reached its crest and was about to plummet downward, Goenka looked up at the boy with a power that shot through him as surely as if it had been a bullet. The fellow stumbled backwards, tripped down the steps and landed in a heap on the ground sobbing, the club lying harmlessly beside him. And what was that power, you may ask? It was love. I saw it clearly. It was love, understanding, concern and complete detachment. Mostly, it was love.

43. *Everyone Needs To Eat*

Since I've been in Canada, and especially since starting work on Sparks Street, I've heard repeatedly that one shouldn't give money to beggars, shouldn't support squeegee kids, and shouldn't feed the pigeons.

I understand not giving money to folks who are obviously having a wee little drinking problem. It's better to give them a sandwich, a nectarine or tickets to the theatre. A street person actually had the audacity recently to stumble into the elegant jewellery shop in which I'm employed. He was drunk. He was, in fact, a drunk. He was also somewhat belligerent. His ragged shirt was untucked, his chin had several days' growth, his sneakers were dirty and untied. He slobbered onto the Rolex counter-top, called out for service in a raspy, demanding voice and openly scratched his lower extremities. I liked him right away.

Unfortunately this is not a perfect world, and I was compelled to try to usher him out as quickly as I could. A few clients there at the time cowered in corners trembling. An elderly lady held a one-and-a-half carat flawless diamond ring in one hand and pointed at the fellow with the other. She muttered something about her tax dollars from the safety of the back showroom, the area where we keep the booze for special clients. Meanwhile, the drunkard had grabbed hold of my lapel and was breathing into my face. He was demanding a diamond ring for his sweetie, wanted to pay not more than a hundred bucks and kept insisting I not cheat him. Of course I couldn't promise that, but I did manage to work my embrace around in such a way as to be in a position to burp him, and I'm sure he felt much better for it.

Eventually, with a promise to keep my eyes open for a ring he could give to the lady in his life, I handed him a business card and sent him out onto Sparks Street. His girlfriend or wife was no doubt waiting faithfully there on one of the benches, unconscious. My colleagues came over to congratulate me on how well I handled the situation, in the course of which the manager said, "You even gave him your business card!" And I replied, "Excuse me, madam. Actually, I gave him one of yours."

And I understand not feeding the pigeons. During my very first lunch hour, thinking it'd be romantic to feed a few crumbs to the pigeons, so many flocked around that it ended up feeling like a Hitchcock film. By the time I walked back into the shop I was traumatised and had pigeon doo-doo all over my new suit.

Squeegee kids are a completely different matter. They're cool. I rather doubt that wiping down windshields while stepping in and out of traffic, breathing the fumes and taking abuse from drivers was their first career choice. And yet, any time I've encountered them, they've been polite and ready to back off without argument. Of course, most people back away from my car. Nevertheless, there are many make-work kind of jobs like that in India; one way or another, you deal with it.

For example, in the latrines of the five star hotels of New Delhi there would always stand a fellow who's only purpose was to hand out little towels. Of course, the towel gig was his way of feeding his wife, six kids, a cow and his aged parents. But, I hated the way he'd watch me do my thing, watch as I wash my hands, then eagerly step forward to hand me a towel for one or two rupees tip. Eventually, I just refused to wash my hands. The attendant would watch me do my thing with that silly smile on his face, watch me shake myself off and tuck myself in. Then, as I'd head for the door, a look of astonishment would replace his smile and I'd say in Hindi, with a strange sense of satisfaction, 'I'm clean.'

A new report, written up in an Ottawa newspaper recently, stated that if homeless youths didn't wipe car windows they'd become involved in crime or the sex trade. And I believe that most intelligent folks can decide whom to give their extra loonies to. So I say, help the squeegee kids and the more unfortunate people around us. Do it for them and do it for yourself. Drunks need food too. And I'd even go so far as to say pigeons need food too. Just don't hang around afterward.

44. It's Good To Be Sure

Some months back, I became reacquainted by chance with a couple that used to be students of mine when I last lived in Canada. That was over nineteen years ago. The Carps had enrolled in my hatha-yoga class at the Jack Purcell Community Centre, evolved into meditation students and became good friends. At least that's the story they told me and they seemed to be sticking to it. I didn't remember them at all. Apparently, I'd even visited their home in Kanata where they still live. So I've decided to stop cooking with aluminium pots or wrapping sandwiches with aluminium foil.

Following our joyous reunion, we caught up with each other's lives over coffee at their place one Sunday in May. The house did seem vaguely familiar. During our little visit, the Carps proudly introduced me to their sixteen-year-old son and nineteen-year-old daughter. The son was a big, strapping lad, but the daughter, though certainly big, seemed a tad on the slow side. I soon realised, while we sipped our tea and chatted, that their daughter was, in fact, quite mentally challenged. The realisation precipitated a subtle sense of uneasiness within me. As I quickly did some calculations, Mrs Carp brought up the fact that she'd been pregnant with her daughter at the time of our meditation classes. I began to squirm a bit in the chair. "As a matter of fact, Nathan," she added in her good natured way while stroking her daughter's cheek, "you predicted at that time that, due to our meditation, this child would be a peaceful soul, and so she is." I reached for a biscuit.

In a life fraught with uncertainties there are a few things of which I'm sure. A waitress at a Chelsea restaurant recently asked if I wanted Earl Grey tea, English Breakfast tea or Orange Pecko tea. It was my personal, direct experience that she said Pecko instead of Pekoe. Nobody can convince me that she didn't say it because I heard Pecko with my own ears.

And I ordered the Orange Pecko tea. I'm sure, for example, that there used to be a certain village near my home in India where only big boulders stand now. I know because I used to walk there often before a flash flood wiped it out. I'm sure my grandfather was a great man. At lunchtime, he'd give each of my friends and myself a nickel for candy, as he'd help us cross the street safely from the school to the shopping centre. He also gave me my first puppy. And I'm sure we come naked into this world. I've seen a few births, and the babies came out totally naked each and every time.

A very young couple came into the shop recently wanting to purchase wedding bands. Of course, since they were just starting out on their married life, they didn't have a pot to you-know-what in, and I really tried to do the best I could for them. A wedding band for him was easily decided upon, and we managed the price, but then we struggled to find a band that suited the girl, with a price that suited their budget. We ran aground, as it were. The fellow, in the meantime, said something I'll remember for a long while, at least until I type it into this machine. The fellow said something you'd have to appreciate, no matter what you think about the institution of marriage or the custom of buying diamond rings and going into debt to mark the blessed occasion. He said something that brought my attention back to the real underlying meaning of marriage in the first place, like helping the poor at Christmas time. "Honestly," he said, "I'd be happy to wear an elastic band on my finger if we can just get a wedding ring that my fiancée really likes." The girl smiled, stroked his knee and moved in closer. And I, with my rusty old monk's heart swelling up like a condom, wanted to move in closer too … only I thought it might be too crowded. It was really their moment. But, I'm sure those two charming kids are in love.

Most of all, in a life fraught with uncertainties, it's good to be sure of at least one important fact. It's good to know something irrefutable due to it being one's own personal experience. Somewhere along the way I experienced directly, as so many people around here seem to have, that we do indeed all come from one source, one ocean of life.

45. The Stuff of Legends

I've heard these hills referred to as one of Eastern Canada's best-kept secrets. I certainly never heard of this area while I was living in India. I heard of Bangkok. There's a girl in Bangkok who can do things with Ping-Pong balls that would almost certainly turn your brown eyes blue. Nice place to visit, of course, but I always had serious doubts about settling down there and raising a family. Not that I'm ready to raise a family here either. I'm still a little young for that.

Had I heard of Wakefield while still in India, I probably wouldn't have run back any earlier. It just would've been nice to know a place like this exists where people were willing to accept a simple guy like me, if not with wide open arms, at least not with rocks and flame-throwers.

The nightlife in Bangkok is more exotic than in Wakefield. I won't lie about that. But, we have one thing Bangkok doesn't have. Phil Jenkins. And these days he's been hosting the bi-monthly Turntable Café at Billy's Restaurant, beside the Black Sheep Inn. He talks, plays and sings a set at the Wednesday night folk-singing sessions before turning over the makeshift stage to guests he invites to join. I was fortunate enough to find out about the sessions, and even offered to donate a box of Ping-Pong balls if needed, though so far Phil seems to have the entertainment well under control.

Last week Phil invited Ian Tamblyn to entertain the crew. And Ian blew us completely away. Although a case could admittedly be made that I've only recently fallen off the turnip truck, I have heard Ian's music before. I even saw him play this last summer at the folk festival in Ottawa. But, there was a special feeling that night, an almost otherworldly sense about his guitar playing and the force of his personality. No major Ottawa news-paper was covering the event, of course. No main-line music or entertainment critic was there. It was an event that slipped through the cracks, mostly unknown, largely forgotten, like the sound of a tree falling way out in the bush somewhere. Only a few of us fortunate folks will remember and perhaps speak of it some day down the road again to kids or old friends, like a microcosmic Woodstock event; 'I was there.'

The only performance I ever saw in India itself that came close to the one we witnessed that night was a one-armed drummer from Aurangabad. It was really quite remarkable what that fellow could do with his one good arm. Talk about wrist action. I did know a one-eyed tailor once, but even though he struck a responsive chord in me, and as skilful as he was in stitching my pyjamas, that's not music. And anyway, to be perfectly honest, he usually made one sleeve longer than the other. Hard to beat that girl with her balls in Bangkok though.

Be that as it may, it would've been enough for Ian to just come to the coffee house and say hello, or have beer, and watch. It would've been a real treat for us to see him go up to the front of the room and, out of a sense of friendship with Phil, sing a song. One or two songs sung routinely would've sufficed. What he did was not only play an extended set, but put his whole soul into each song as though he were at the Troubadour in Los Angeles. He voiced each lyric as though he'd just written it or just lived it, and he left no doubt that he doesn't care a fig for name, fame and certainly not money really when it comes right down to true folk artistry. His craft is all-important. What he did was show the lucky ones there in that little room last Wednesday evening that he likes Phil and what he's about, the sound in the room, and the people of this village. Mostly, what Ian did was just continue to live the moments of his life as he is.

Sitting near the front, I could clearly understand why the Phil Jenkins and Ian Tamblyns of today's Gatineau Hills will be the folk legends of tomorrow's generations. They'd give up a hundred 'normal' days for a few days fully lived, a few songs masterfully written and sung.

46. There's Something About A Man In Uniform

Standing in line at the Banque Nationale can be tricky. I was once accused, while patiently waiting to cash my weekly poverty-level pay cheque, of being sexist in my writing. I didn't even know what the word meant. Of course, it sounded similar to racist so I pretended that I hadn't written the column in question. I just kept insisting there had been a terrible mistake.

Just the other day, while accessing the cash machine for nearly my last twenty dollars, I was accused of having a penile complex. At first I thought that meant I was afraid of going to jail, which seemed reasonable to me. In fact, I thanked the lady. Only, then she explained that this column deals with the functions of the penile appendage far too often for her liking. I not only believe that to be a lie, I want to go on record as having categorically denied it. In fact, I strongly resent that.

Enough said on that topic. I'd actually like to mention something about my hockey career. It began when I was just a wee little willy wanker of about twelve. Growing up outside of Toronto, as I like to think I did, playing hockey was just something one was supposed to do. Unfortunately, I wasn't a very good skater. It's hard to pick up much speed when you skate on your ankles. Too much friction. In some activities friction's a good thing; in others it's a bad thing. You know what I mean.

My parents paid good money to enrol me in a local intramural hockey league. It must've been good money because the coach seemed to feel compelled to let me play. He tried me out at centre, and that didn't work out at all. He moved me to one wing and then to another, one defence and then another, until I eventually landed a spot in goal. The very night that I was to play goalie just happened to be the coldest of the winter. And those years were a lot colder than these. Well I got all suited up with layer upon layer of protective clothing and padding, including that little metal cup covering my genitals, and waddled out onto the ice.

I felt very alone standing in the goal so far away from where all the other players gathered to begin the game. I felt alone, and I could hear my little heart thumping away inside my padded chest. I could also feel my little bladder and got a sinking feeling when I realised I had to pee. I wondered how I was supposed to take care of that need without spending a half-hour time-out to remove all that stuff, drain my lizard, and then put it all back on again.

Pretty much the first play of the game was a breakaway by the other team. From the face-off, one of their more goon-like players, who in retrospect I believe must've lied about his age, skidded down the ice towards me. I had to pee. Our defence-men were left flatfooted at the blue line as that train-wreck of an opponent bore down on me, inexorably closer, closer, closer, as I stood my ground. With one simple fake in front of the goal he shot, I peed, he scored, and I nearly froze my penile off as I later walked home.

47. *Leaving On A Jet Plane*

D uring the fall of 1978 I decided to leave India forever. It wasn't because of anything said or done to me. I simply wasn't having a good time, and I couldn't imagine living there any longer. The fact that I had malaria at the time, however, may have contributed to my sorry state of mind.

I was stuck up in my cabin on the hillside far from the hermitage. Once or twice each day someone would look in on me and bring some food that I wouldn't eat. Otherwise, I'd be alone with a fever that made me sweat profusely, chills that made me shake uncontrollably, medicine that made me retch, and thoughts that made me miserable. Of course I cursed my decision to go to Bombay, where I had contracted the disease, and I cursed my decision to live so far from everyone I knew. Most of all, however, I couldn't understand why Swamiji, my best friend and teacher, hadn't sent even one message in the whole two weeks of my illness; I wanted to leave once and forever.

Malaria is a rather unpleasant experience, but Quinine just might be worse. It became more and more difficult to face that big monster pill each day. My mood became darker than the monsoon skies outside until, on the tenth and last day of my medicine, I'd had just about enough. Rain poured down through the night, and I was alone with the last pill. It was just that last pill and me. Swamiji didn't care and no one would know that I never took it. So I placed it under my bed in a glass and rolled over.

The night was wild. Even though I avoided the horrible effects of the Quinine, I couldn't really sleep. The dramatic storm raging all around kept me awake. At just about eleven thirty, one of my friends walked in the front door soaked to the skin, and I remarked that he must've been mad to trudge all the way up to see me in that storm. He agreed. He said that he never would've come had he not been sent directly by Swamiji to deliver a note. I was shocked. It was the very first acknowledgement that he even knew I was ill. I was even more shocked, however, after I read it.

Dearest Nathan,

Take your last pill and you'll be better by the morning.

Love, Swamiji.

I reached under my bed for the pill, swallowed it, with some difficulty, with some water, and I was up and around by the morning.

It wasn't until about two years later that I ever had another thought to leave. Swamiji called me up to talk in front of two hundred and fifty people, which in itself was not a problem. But, he gave me the topic of relationships. That's just not a topic I can speak on with any authority. The best relationship I ever had had been with a basketball. All I really know is you can't make someone love you. You can only stalk them and hope they panic and give in. Be that as it may, I began my speech that day having decided to tell a funny story about my aunt Fay, who had a deuce of a time finding a husband. She finally did find a husband, I continued, which pleased the family tremendously. It eventually became obvious, however, that all was not well with my aunt Fay and uncle Morris. They seemed to be having trouble starting a family. We presumed they knew how to go about it, but not even a mouse came out. When, however, my aunt did become pregnant, or as was said in those days, had a bun in the oven, the whole family rejoiced. And finally I related how, after the usual nine months, my aunt gave birth to a child severely mentally challenged.

At that point I realised my story wasn't the least bit funny. In fact, I'm sure you'll agree it was in rather bad taste. There was total silence except for a few gasps and moans. Then Swamiji turned to me and said with a big grin upon his face, "Are you sure that wasn't your mother?" The crowd went wild. Their laughter nearly tore the roof off the hall, and I went home straight afterwards to pack. But I didn't leave India that time either; and, in fact, I've realised over the years that my cousin Bobby happens to be the one member of my family who really seems to understand me.

48. Special

Having finished the day, the week and the shopping year on Sparks Street, my co-workers and I, along with the owners of the store in which we collect daily, toasted the coming of the new millennium. Then I drove back to Wakefield and settled in for the night. I watched Lloyd Robertson host a show that scanned the globe.

To me, Lloyd looks as though he employs a sculptor rather than a barber. But, I watched in awe as folks all over the world celebrated like hungry, wild tribes people after a long-awaited kill. I was enthralled with the number of engagements publicly announced at midnight, captivated by a couple French-kissing repeatedly on international television to herald in the new age, and moved, yet again, by the deep love between Celine Dion and her husband. Celine's joyous father traipsed around the stage of his daughter's televised concert kissing people even though he looked as though he'd have been more comfortable squeezing maple syrup out of a back-yard tree to mark the occasion.

For me, it felt just fine, this time, to watch a little television, shovel some white stuff from my driveway, go for a walk up Rockhurst, take a bath, and go to bed. In the morning I finished the shovelling; and, when I came back inside, there was a message waiting on my answering machine. It was from my mommy. "Nathan, this is your mother calling," she began, "I just wanted to wish you a Happy New Year. I sure hope you had a better time last night than your father and I. All we did was watch television, go for a short walk, take a bath and go to bed." And as odd as it may have felt to realize I celebrated the coming year and new millennium in exactly the same fashion as my eighty-five year old parents, I rather hoped my mom's bathing comment wasn't quite the way it sounded. That just was not an image I was emotionally prepared to accept.

In years gone by, in India, my New Year's celebrations were more or less the same as here, with much less snow. I do remember one in particular, however, when my teacher decided he wanted to travel up to the higher reaches of the mountains for the day. Needless to say, we all piled in whatever cars we could find to follow. We stopped along the way, and he spoke at length about the significance of the year ending and the new one just about to begin. At one point in the day, after walking through snow in his bare feet, Swami asked me to help put his shoes and socks on while he continued to talk to the crowd. While he leaned against a tree, I put one sock on and then the other. I put one shoe on, tried to put the second on, but I ran into trouble.

All the while, Swami was talking about the significance of a new year while I struggled with that shoe. He talked of the importance of meditation on our common source, our true self, our eternal self, living more for others, a little less for one's individual self alone, contemplation on the one life permeating all, good stuff like that. Meanwhile, I was pressing his little foot into the sneaker while he pushed down on my hands. And just as he was exclaiming that this was to be 'Nathan's year,' he stamped down so hard he forced my hands right to the ground and mashed them into a large paddy of cow dung.

All the way back to town, as I bumped along in the back seat of the taxi, I thought about what happened there. I wondered what it meant to have the whole new year dedicated to me at the same time as having my hands smudged all around a heaping, steaming pile of smelly cow stuff. I don't remember anything special or unusual happening that year. And I don't necessarily expect anything special to happen this year. I've come to understand that having the company of so many good people as I do around here, being able to still chew and digest food, being able to cherish this life is quite special enough.

49. The Breath of Life

Finally, having been busy seven days a week for what felt like ever, it was Christmas. Unfortunately, predictably, having reached a precious two days off in a row, I was sick. Every single soul at the shop had the nasty flu that grabbed most of Ottawa and outlying areas by our collective throat.

I was feeling stranger by the minute on the run up to Christmas. I recall standing with a fever and a client, trying to talk about the sparkly engagement ring he wanted to present to his sparkly girlfriend on New Year's Eve. He appeared to turn into an Orangutang right in front of my red eyes. One moment he was a computer geek trying to start the millennium off with a bang, and the next moment he seemed to turn into an ape, pounding his chest and scratching his ankles without even bending down. He was chortling, showing his teeth, and making suggestive hip thrusts towards the Gucci watch cabinet, and I decided it was time to go home.

On the way, I stopped in at the Wakefield hospital and waited with most of the village for a doctor to tell me the obvious. When one finally did get round to me it was two days later, and I had Pneumonia. Well, actually it was still the same evening, only much later, and I was delirious. The doctor was very nice and thorough, and he confidently told me I probably could avoid antibiotics with a week or two of complete rest, vapour inhalations and lots of herb teas. I looked up at him gratefully, thanked him warmly and said "Doc, give me the friggin drugs!" Quite frankly, I'd have gone in for chemotherapy right about then.

I've seen a few epidemics in my day. There was the great cholera epidemic of 1981, which you probably never heard of, in Uttar Pradesh. At the time, I was on a pilgrimage of sorts to the source of the holy Ganges River north of a village called Utkarshi. I was told by an official-looking fellow at the provincial border post that I could enter the area only at my own risk which, correct me if I'm wrong, is usually the case. Would it really matter who was held responsible if my carcass was discovered lying bloated by the side of the dusty road somewhere in India's northern regions? Certainly not to me. In any event, I was quite confident that my tremendous religious merit would keep me safe and in good stead. I was very religious back then. Now I'm merely spiritual, so I would have to now avoid cholera areas. And, except for a severe case of indigestion brought on by ingesting a bit too much curry one evening, it seemed to prove true.

Over the years I have witnessed, and fallen victim to, epidemics of hepatitis, gastritis, malaria and spring fever, the last being by far the most dangerous. In 1994, there was a memorable outbreak of the Pneumonic Plague in Gujarat, which you may actually have heard about. It began in a charming little town called Surat that, of course, was immediately nicknamed Sewerat. The Pneumonic Plague is a close relation to the Bubonic plague and every bit as nasty. Hundreds of people died within a couple of days, and over two hundred and fifty thousand fled the city. The village elders, for some reason, didn't want people to leave; although I have no doubt that many of those same elders slithered out during the night. The Gujarati health minister went on nation-wide television to reassure the population that there was no need to panic. He was, unfortunately, having a really bad hair day. It was sticking up in all directions. He looked tired, drawn, unkempt. In fact, he looked as though he had the Pneumonic Plague. Meanwhile, he implored everyone to stay calm and to stay home; he ended with the line "Soon, the situation will most certainly be under control." Which meant, of course, that the situation was completely, totally out of control. A very wise if somewhat morose Buddhist monk I once knew in Dharmsala used to say that life was like a disease with a bad prognosis. The prognosis, presumably, being death. My teacher, Swami Shyam, often says in many ways that life never ends. Whichever way you choose to approach this human situation, one truth stands tall: breath is a precious gift, the gift of life. I try to remember that as I go about my daily tasks, back at full strength. Of course, I may never be able to look at that Gucci cabinet quite the same again.

50. Lotus Notes or
Don't Try This At Home

From 1969 to 1974 I had been meditating as a Vipassana, Buddhist monk within the lineage of U Ba Kin from Burma. During retreats, we were strictly silent with no eye contact, reading, writing or exercising, other than a little stretching. We ate modest, vegetarian meals at six and eleven in the morning and tea and fruit in the afternoon. Needless to say, I never missed a meal.

Sometime in 1970, at an old Jesuit retreat centre in the Sierra-Nevada Mountains. California, about fifty of us had been meditating for thirty-one days. There were only two days left, and we were three hours into a four-hour vow to sit in one-pointed concentration on the breath. I can only assume that my attention span has deteriorated since then. The other night, I was trying to watch a program on television about Attention Deficit Disorder; but the host was taking way too long to get to the point, so I switched to the hockey game. During the days of the retreat to which I've referred, however, I was still an eager beaver. I even sat in a full lotus posture the whole time.

For the uninitiated, I should explain that the full lotus position is very much like sitting cross-legged, except that one twists one's legs like a pretzel so that each foot rests on its opposite thigh. Were I to try it tonight, you'd most certainly recognise me walking sideways toward the Wakefield hospital in the morning with a sour look on my face. I've long since realised that pain and suffering is not the best way for a human being to grow. I encourage people to always meditate in as comfortable a position as they can without falling dead asleep or drooling into their laps. But, that retreat was at a different time, and I was of a different mind.

The gong had been struck to signal the start of the last hour, and I was tremendously hopeful of great insights and great progress because, you see, I was in excruciating pain. As time went on, though I still felt I might soon experience something extra-normal, I also began to think I might die or be crippled forever after. I began to feel like Wily Coyote, a character out of the old Road Runner cartoons, trying, but helplessly watching the edge zoom inexorably closer, digging his heels into the ground with no real effect.

I'm not at all sure I could've put a halt to my slide even had I decided I wanted to. I was, in effect, locked into position by then. Yet it's quite true that at that moment I made a definite decision to go on all the way, to see what lay beyond the edge, to jump off into the unknown. The pain and the heat in my body had been building, to use another analogy, like a pressure cooker. When the pressure finally released, however, it was not overtly dramatic. It was more of a flowering- gentle, incredibly exquisite. And my consciousness, released from its confined, uncomfortable prison cell, wafted upwards, in a manner of speaking, out of my body. No more pressure. No more pain. And we had all transcended together. One consciousness. One life.

A truck drove up the drive and we could see it. The curtains on all the windows were closed, but we still watched the driver slam the door of his van and lumber up to the hall. He was a plumber. I could see the printing on his van and a long ladder on the side. The stout fellow knocked on the door and called out "Hello. Hello," even while looking down at all the shoes and involuntarily sensing the pervasive silence. The growing look of panic upon his face made me want to laugh as we watched him stumble quickly back down the stairs, jump into his truck and drive off.

The next forty minutes passed quickly. Periodically, when my body would sufficiently cool I would filter back as a birth until the pressure and heat and pain would force me out again. I vividly recall the sound of the gong at the end of the four hours. It was a lovely sound, far away, irrelevant, yet lovely. And when I eventually untucked my legs and walked out into the mid-afternoon sun, slowly and carefully at first, I knew I had changed.

51. The Second Winter

Winter, as lovely as it is here in Wakefield, does present certain problems, many of which are still new to me. What do I know, for example, about shovelling snow? Really. The only stuff I had to shovel in India was not white or fluffy. And for the most part I merely stepped around it. I certainly never had to clear any off the roof with an extension pole before the roof caved in.

This is my second winter here in Canada, in Wakefield. I went right out last year and proudly bought a sparkling, brand new shovel before the first fluffy flakes flew. It didn't take long, however, to realize I was attacking an army with an airgun, so to speak. Only much later did I hear that one really must have a larger, scoop-type shovel if one doesn't have a blower or, better yet, a plough attached to one's truck. A backhoe would not be out of place, but then you all know that.

With winter approaching this year my old car broke down for the umpteenth time and, as a certain friend of mine likes to say, I panicked. I'm not sure that's entirely fair, however, since each time it bottomed out the cost was nearly what I paid for the thing in the first place. That last time my '87 Toyota and I grumbled together into a garage, it was going to cost even more so I told the boys I wasn't going to spend another rupee on it. I told them to put it back together with duct tape if necessary. Then I chugged out to Broom Chrysler Plymouth Jeep What-Have-You and pounced on the first vehicle that would make me look like I had a big ... wallet. What do I know about mechanics? Unlike everyone else around here, along with his brother, sister and grandmother, I'm mechanically challenged. I hadn't owned a car in over twenty-eight years.

The new car, although fully loaded, did not come with snow tires. That fact only dawned on me during one of the recent blizzards, somewhere around Pine Road. And I've come to understand that All-Season tires means all seasons except winter in Wakefield if you're planning to go out at all before spring, which I didn't last year. Unfortunately, I'm not real eager to spend another five hundred to one thousand dollars on tires, or tires with rims, just now. I spent so much on the basic car itself that I'll probably be a slave to 'the system' until I'm so old that I become one of those codgers who can't turn their necks to see if any car's coming before changing lanes. And anyway, so far the only time I've ever really missed having snow tires was when I was skidding totally out of control down a snow-covered Rockhurst Avenue straight for the car ahead or the river. At least the heater works.

Having shifted to a larger, meaning normal-sized house this year, the oil bills have shifted also. The furnace uses so much oil I believe the Morrison's might just as well leave the tanker parked in my driveway. What do I know about furnaces? The homes in India were traditionally built with really thick, stone and mud walls, tiny windows and heavy slate roofs. A few candles could heat the place. The family quarters were built on the top floor with the animals down below, the theory being that if the river were to flood, the family cow, goat and pig would be the first to go. In the meantime, there was no doubt a lot of fur flying on those frigid winter nights.

I'm not one of those folks who walk around outside grinning when it's minus forty-seven with wind-chill. I'm not one of those folks who stammer, 'you can dress for the cold, but not for the heat. You can dress for the cold, but not for the heat,' incessantly. Nevertheless, whatever hardships lurk just under the snow of winter, I do enjoy a good skate on the Rideau Canal. Half way to Dow's Lake from Fifth Avenue and one Beaver Tail later, on my first time out this season, I realised how much more at home and settled I feel this year as compared to last. And there's nothing quite like the snow-cloud heaven of a wintry Wakefield full-moon night. Of course, I can't help feeling sorry for all those people who've been advised by their doctors to stay away from salt.

52. All Systems Go

Having lived in this western wonderland now for almost two years, I have noticed a few small ironies. Hardly anything worth mentioning, perhaps, but it does seem to me that this capitalist system, driven as it is by a free-market economy, better known as greed, does have its quirks.

I'm sure you'll agree, for example, that a schedule that does not allow you to spend a reasonable amount of time out in the light of day is in need of some reconsideration. To trundle off to one's place of employment, in the winter months, as the sun is just showing its glorious countenance over the horizon, only to return home zombie-like and slightly mummified after dark, day after day, is simply crazy. In fact, I'm surprised more good people don't end up totally barking mad.

Perhaps I'm wrong. Lord knows I haven't the qualifications usually attached to a person considered worth listening to. I haven't a PhD, I'm not rich, and I don't subscribe to the Globe and Mail. I prefer The Low Down to Hull and Back News, as a matter of fact. I'm just a normal fellow who likes to get out and smell the roses, enjoys good old family values, strolls along these peaceful village lanes, or puts on a simple black dress and heels for a night on the town every now and again. But even me, a single person with no kids, dogs or amoebas, finds it hard to find time or energy to do the things I enjoy.

There was a documentary on television, one evening last week, all about the pervasive problem of sleep deprivation. People are just too damned tired. They're falling asleep all over the place; at work, in cafes, on buses. And when the program began to discuss the possibility of scheduled nap times in the middle of the workday as a solution, I laughed out loud and turned it off. Firstly, it won't happen. Secondly, the sleepy-time rooms would no doubt be as airless as the office that knocked the people out to begin with. Thirdly, nap time misses the point entirely. Rather, it's attempting to solve the problem with more of the same problems. The whole day is already fully scheduled, including sleep. There's a total disregard for the natural rhythms of the life. And fourthly, I had to go to bed.

During a break from a very intense day at work recently, I wandered around a bit in order to ingest some semi-fresh air, had a bite to eat in a semi-palatable restaurant, then sat on a semi-comfortable, padded bench in the building where the restaurant was. Eventually, I lay down on the bench. But, even though I was dressed in shirt and tie, even though the bench was quite out of the main part of the building, a security officer came and demanded I sit up. I had to sit up! I was not even allowed to recline. Indignant, I pulled my pants back up, put my shoes on and left the building.

As India happily embraces all things western, the people gallop toward their own new-found wealth and suffer the consequences. In days gone by, however, Indians were free. They could lie where they fell or talk uninhibitedly with any stranger near at hand without fear. They could also relieve their bladder into any bush that looked good, but that may be why most of the Indian Deccan is now almost totally devoid of vegetation. Still today, the ways of old often persist, as evidenced by the wandering mendicants traipsing up and down the country barefoot, wearing only loincloths and a silly grin, and total strangers using your shoulder for a pillow while sleeping away a bus ride. Village India had its drawbacks as well. But, at least you could wear what you liked and lie down under the sky when you felt the need.

The most immediate way to change this system, or the world, is still to change oneself. It's a personal work to learn simple living and higher thinking. Creating a life replete with fresh air and a few rays of sunlight just might be the ticket. Having said all that, I must add that most of the great thinkers through the ages have talked, written, and, in many cases, transcended their limitations. From Sri Aurobindo and Mahatma Gandhi all the way to the likes of Hurricane Carter, humankind has realised, or at least glimpsed, the fact that ultimately no system, jail or body can really bind the true self.

53. Jaipur

Just last week, I was doing some inventory in the elegant shop on Sparks Street in which I'm presently employed. I was sitting at my desk, near the fake fireplace that exudes a kind of fake cosiness, when a lady walked in wearing a fake fur coat, a fake smile, and she began to browse around. But, even though I watched her I wasn't really there. I was in the Indian heartland, in Rajasthan. And the year was 1983.

Having begun my business in the mountains, I used to go on periodic buying trips to the major lapidary centres, such as Agra or Jaipur, fairly often. And in those days I was not very sophisticated in how I went about it. Since the assassination of Indira Gandhi, the official attitude toward foreigners had changed. Canada was accused of harbouring Sikh Kalhistani separatists, and I had forgotten my passport. That was not a good combination. I also did not have enough bank receipts to cover the amount of rupees I was carrying, and I was carrying far too much jewellery in my bag. On top of those mistakes, I filled in all the spaces of the register at the hotel as closely as I could recall, but I left the space for visa number blank. Had I written any number at all I'd have been all right. The police, however, were checking hotels daily, and they saw that I was both Canadian and had no visa number. I was in trouble. The hotel was in trouble.

Returning to the hotel that hot afternoon with a large case full of money and jewellery, and no proper papers whatsoever, I encountered a lobby full of freaked out hotel people. Apparently the police had been there. I tried to get them to let me fill in the blank, but it was far too late for that. They insisted I accompany them down to the police station. It occurred to me that trotting off to see the local gendarme would probably mean the end of my business, if not my stay in India, if not indeed my personal freedom.

While these unsettling thoughts quickly flitted through my mind, a crowd gathered; and the discussion went from bad to worse. The hoteliers became progressively more frantic, loud and aggressive. Since I'd never stayed there before, I didn't know anyone at all. At one point the manager grabbed my arm, and I'm afraid I don't do well with people grabbing me at the best of times. I pulled my arm away and said something uncomplimentary about his mother. He grabbed me again, harder. Then I lost my composure. I panicked. I pushed him into the crowd and ran like hell, lugging my heavy case along. Ignoring the 42-degree scorching heat, I tore through the streets with at least four men on my heels. They were yelling. I could hear their footsteps, though I dared not look behind. Twisting and turning through the thick market, I ran like the devil until I made yet another mistake. I ran straight into a blind alley. I was trapped. I looked around wildly for any way out, a place to run, somewhere to hide.

Then, a remarkable thing happened. An old lady, dressed in the meanest of rags, whistled to me. She motioned for me to crawl in to a kind of small garage in amongst tires and old cans. Once inside, some children, as unclean and unkempt as the lady, threw jute bags on top of me before continuing on with their games as though nothing unusual was happening. The old lady swept around the entrance. And, as the men ran up to the lane, I actually saw her pointing onward. After a few long minutes the children uncovered me and helped shove me over a stone and mud wall. I swallowed some dirt as I clawed my way over and dropped down into what appeared to be an entirely new market. I hopped into a scooter, choking, coughing, gasping for air, and told the driver to head for Gangotri Bazaar. I had escaped. I could hardly believe what had happened in that alley, and I never thanked that lady or those kids.

"Excuse, me. Do you work here?" I looked up to see the lady with the fake fur. She was asking me to show her a strand of pearls. I was back. Still, as I fastened a strand around the lady's well-oiled neck, a part of me was still hiding in that alley in Jaipur. A part of me always will be, I suppose.

54. Hold Onto Your Pants

To those of you who follow this column weekly, I'm grateful and concerned about you both. I mean I'm both grateful and concerned about you. Be that as it may, you're the ones who'll recall the story I narrated last time about my close encounter with the Jaipur police. And you will no doubt be mortified to read that that was not, in fact, the end of the story.

Having narrowly escaped an Indian lynch mob and the Indian penal system, for the moment, I took a scooter to the home of a business acquaintance and hunkered down there for the next couple days. He and his family took good care of me. They spared no effort to make me comfortable, help me to feel at home and reassure me that all would be right in the end. Of course, I was dropping nearly fifty thousand rupees into the family coffers through my business, but I like to think they really cared. Although fifty-thousand rupees is hardly enough for a cappuccino and carrot cake at Chapters, it's a couple months' worth of veggies and chapattis for a large family or a small village in India.

After completing our business, we ate a meal to celebrate, and then my friend and his family sent me on my way happily. I mean they sent me happily on my way. The huge crowd at the Interstate Bus terminal, however, made it impossible for me to get to the ticket counter until a man, with an impressive handlebar moustache, took an interest in helping. As the friendly fellow ran interference for me, I managed to claw my way to the counter and acquire a ticket. I was terribly grateful for his help.

Still, somewhat paranoid, I moved to the opposite side of the street to watch the loading of the bus from a safe distance. And, as I watched from a doorway across the road, I saw that same man with the handlebar moustache ride up on a police jeep. With several officers hanging off the vehicle, fingering their holsters and swinging their big sticks, he was pointing excitedly to the bus for New Delhi.

My lower extremities dissolved. The scene in front of me unfolded as if in slow motion. As the police began searching the bus, the driver's registry and the surrounding area, I slid to the ground and caterpillared away. I beat another hasty retreat through another alley to another street, jumped into another rickshaw and scooted back to the same old house of my friends. They appeared somewhat less than enthusiastic to see me so soon again. Still, they let me in, quickly closed the door and, obviously not into reminiscing about the good old days, spirited me out of town soon after dusk. I was dropped off unceremoniously at the side of a dark highway to catch local buses all the way to New Delhi. But, I was free. The matter never came up again, except once.

After that ill-fated trip to 'The Pink City,' I sorely regretted having to leave behind a certain pair of jeans in the hotel room there. I had been fiercely attached to those pants. They were western, fit like a glove, had faded beautifully, even had patches on the knees, and they were Levis. I'd been in India a long time.

Six months later, it so happened that I returned to Jaipur again on business. My girlfriend accompanied me, and I felt sure there wouldn't be any trouble. In reality, I was obsessing over those pants; and, in retrospect, wonder if I really even had to go to Jaipur at all. I couldn't resist. Once there, I devised a bold, brave and gallant plan. We'd take a scooter to that hotel, my lady would enter and demand her boyfriend's lost Levi pants. I would keep a watch on the proceedings from my scooter. As it turned out, while I watched I saw my plan unravel horribly as more and more people gathered. I even saw one of the hotel workers slip away and run obviously toward the police station.

Needless to say, we were fortunate to get away with our shorts. As my partner jumped aboard the scooter in a near panic, disillusioned with my plan and perhaps with me, the men began to move ominously toward us. They were collectively frowning, except for one boy standing off to the side who was actually smiling. And, as I looked back through the little rear window, I realised why. He was wearing my pants.

55. Simple Living and Higher Thinking

Never before in the history of humankind has there been such a pressure to look good. There's never been as strong an emphasis on staying in shape or on remaining young and nubile. That creates a certain problem. Because, aside from having to figure out how to halt the ageing process, there's office work, television, movies, Internet, junk food and order-in Sweet and Sour Chicken Balls to contend with. Consequently, there's also never been a population so sedentary or so full of sloth and torpor.

Of course, I have absolutely no facts or figures to back up my hypotheses. And so it's only fair to add that there's also never been so many fitness centres. I'm equally unsure of that fact, but I visited the YM/YWCA once since returning to Canada, mostly hoping to shoot a few jump shots, and got involved in a pick-up game that was nearly the death of me. The guys were very young, very big and very skilful, which is a combination I resent. Later the same evening, while watching 'Who Wants To Be A Jerk?', eating a Sandy's Pizza, drinking a beer, scratching my belly and soaking my head with ice, I realised I quite like being slothful. I feel good that way. Some of my best friends are slothful. But, I'm also afraid to just let myself go.

So, next I visited the 'Good Life' fitness centre, which implies that if you join up you'll finally have a good life. Situated in the bowels of the Rideau Centre, it was so crowded I couldn't help but wonder if there was enough oxygen being pumped in. People of all shapes and sizes occupied machines of all shapes and sizes squeezed tight against each other. While using the machines, one can hook up to another machine that measures one's heart rate. One can wear earphones and listen to one's music of choice even while non-stop music pounds through the place anyway. One can hook a vibrator up to one's genitalia so as not to leave any of the senses unstimulated. I'm not entirely sure about the last one. I just wouldn't be surprised.

An attendant was called on to give me a tour of the place. The fellow turned out to be a huge, hunky stud-muffin, which I rather thought would demoralise any normal sized man with a weaker self-image than myself. I was fine, of course. No Problem with me. I just kept passing comments like, "If I join, do I get free steroids so I can look like you?" or, "Do they use your photo for the 'after' shot?" or, "You think you're so smart, don't you?" The tour lasted about five minutes, the place really being the size of my bedroom anyway, and the attendant walked away shaking his head, poor sport. Anyway, the 'pay schedule' was so complicated I would've had to send it to my brother, the accountant, to figure it out. My mortgage contract was more understandable and I don't understand it after three years.

I have not one, not two, but several friends who've either had cancer, brain tumours or died. The odd part is that none of them smoked, drank, ate wrong or partied hard. And then there's the case of Winston Churchill, who drank like a fish and smoked forever. My mom's been smoking for as long as I've known her, has had a questionable diet and at the age of eighty-two, though admittedly with a face like the map of Vermont, still golfs, swims, plays tennis and takes no guff from anyone except me, 'cause I'm special.

Once, not too long ago during a family funeral, a lady nobody seemed to know watched my mom pull out a ciggy; she commented, "Oh, you still smoke, do you?" Anyone in the room who was at all familiar with my mom took a deep breath and began to pray. "Yes I do," was all mom said in response. We all thought she showed unusual restraint. Of course, it was a sacred occasion. "That can't be doing you much good." We couldn't believe the lady was continuing. Uncles and aunts were sneaking away. There was a long silence during which my brother and I looked over at each other. Mom was breathing hard, holding herself back. And then the unthinkable happened. The silly old lady said, "Have you ever tried to quit?" Mom threw her arms up in the air, jumped out of the sofa and barked, "Have you ever tried to mind your own business!?" All manner of folks were running out of the room holding their stomachs. My brother and I just rolled our eyes.

Next week I'll continue this one-sided discussion with a terribly uplifting moral. But, for now, I'll end as though there's no sense to be made of this strange phenomenon called Life. Be well.

56. Pee Soup

One of my best friends had an operation several years ago to remove a nasty tumour from a sensitive part of his anatomy. After the procedure, as he regained consciousness, he looked up at the nurse and asked if it was a boy or a girl. Another friend, as he was being wheeled into an operating room not very long ago, opened his eyes and asked his wife what was happening. She told him that the doctors were going to operate on his brain. He looked over at his son, smiled and said, 'I guess I'd better organise my thoughts." I myself had an intrusive procedure done to remove many of my tonsils, years back, and as I came to I looked over at my mom and said, "Aargh! Augh! Don't forget you promised me ice cream after! Augh! Aargh!"

Who knows why some of us special ones find a strength and a fearlessness when facing danger. Some of us must just be born with an innate awareness that we're greater than this mortal coil. Whether one is more or less unencumbered by the fear attached to the body's inevitable demise, whether we have an idea of what God is, we all at least hope we'll have someone we can turn to in times of need. Who looks out for us? Parents, of course, try to shelter us from life's little stings. Friends come in handy at times. Doctors can be dangerous, but they're well meaning. The police are here to serve and protect.

That's why I felt so good to hear, as I cooled my heels on the Macdonald Cartier bridge one morning last week in rush hour, that the police were checking seat belts. At first I thought the hold-up must've been precipitated by a horrific accident. Then I wondered if it might not be the truckers on a righteous crusade. So when I heard, on the radio, that the Quebec police were hoping to force an increase in their pay by holding us for over an hour while performing the safety checks, I felt totally, hysterically reassured. The warm, fuzzy feeling that came from knowing we were all being inconvenienced for our own good was tempered only slightly by the fact that I eventually had to urinate so badly my stomach hurt. Anyone looking in at me would've thought I was really grooving to the music. Having a bladder the size of a walnut does not really mesh with police protests on the bridge during rush hour.

Eventually, it became obvious that I had to make a decision. I could get out of my car and piddle on the side of the highway in clear view of all the other hostages or I could piddle into a half-full (half-empty?) jar of steamed vegetables I'd brought for lunch. I chose to sacrifice my lunch in favour of saving myself a greater embarrassment. I unbuckled the seatbelt, knowing full well that the police might find their way to my car at that precise moment to check if I was buckled up. Then they'd really have something to protest. I wondered if God could be so cruel, knowing full well that He could. Still, I unzipped my pants, draped my little brother over the lip of the jar and proceeded to change those steamed vegetables into steaming veggie soup with miso. I'd love to write how I had potato, pee and leak soup for lunch. But, actually I threw the stuff away as soon as I finally arrived. Still, I had that sense of well being which comes from knowing the police were really there for us.

An Israeli friend of mine was living in Canada when his mother fell ill back in Israel. He stayed in close contact with the hospital, and one day the doctor phoned from Israel to report that he best get there right away if he wanted to see his mother before she died. So my friend jumped on a plane, flew to Israel and sat at his mother's bedside. He took hold of her hand and, although she'd been in a coma for more than a day, opened her eyes to look at her eldest son. And her very last words were "Oye. If you've come I really must be dying." In the end, we die alone. Or perhaps we never die. There's a wise old saying in India that goes; 'There may appear to be many separate waves rising and falling, but it's all one ocean.'

57. Zen and The Art of Darts, or Recaptured Moments

Hardly a couple of weeks ago, during a short meeting around a long table at the famous Black Sheep Inn, News staffers gathered to discuss the meaning of life.

We knew it was darts night. Nikki valiantly volunteered to take the chair closest to the action, leaving her upper torso most vulnerable. And I occupied the other chair on the same side because her body shielded mine. Still, though we believed ourselves to be far enough to the side, one of the dartists approached. "Sorry to bother youse guys," he started. "But, I'd hates to see youse get a dart in the neck or something, aye? Hows 'bout youse moving just over to the left there, aye?" And so we did. You bet. But, it was really unnecessary. Any of youse guys who've ever had the pleasure of watching the Wednesday night dart players knows their high level of skill. Some of them have the feathered touch of surgeons. I haven't seen wrist action like that since Earl the Pearl Munro played basketball for the Knicks.

I have no idea if it was Billy's fried zucchinis, the quarter glass of white wine or the atmosphere in the place, but I began to have an 'extra normal' experience. When the pulse in my head and heart grow disproportionate to my surroundings or activity level, and people throwing darts are transformed into beings of light – a cosmic perfection mirrored by the expertise of their throws – that's darned extra-normal, and I automatically became reflective.

Back in 1976, during a six-month silent meditation retreat in the south of India, the days and nights blended together like so many unnoticed breaths. And, with hardly a few weeks remaining, my teacher U. S. N. Goenka beckoned me to the front of the hall. He told me to sit facing him, and there we meditated together for some time.

Any technique I may have been using soon became superfluous. I felt myself sailing far away, into a vast ocean of consciousness. I had no idea how long it had been when I heard Goenka clear his throat and suggest I open my eyes. But, when I opened them I couldn't see him at all. Where he was supposed to be, where I'd left him, was a brilliant light. And rays were shooting from out of a mass of swirling atoms somewhere in the centre. "Can you see the centre?" I heard him ask. I said I could. I could see it with eyes open or closed and I could feel it continuously. "From now on," he said, "you meditate on that centre. Imagine ripples of good will spreading outward, filling your body, the room, the universe and back again."

So the days and nights passed gradually until it was suddenly time to leave. I wasn't the least bit sorry. I'd known for a long time that I wanted most of all to return to the hermitage in the mountains. At the very conclusion of the retreat, I waited outside Goenka's cottage. I was ready to tell him my plans, though mostly to thank him and say good-bye. But I didn't get very far. As I began telling him about Swami Shyam he barked, "I'm sure he's a very nice man, but you can't do both!" Then he puffed up his chest and marched purposefully towards his car. Those last moments were not going at all the way I'd envisioned. I tried to keep up beside him, still hoping to have a few more words until I smashed smack into the trunk of a tree so hard that I fell flat on my backside. Goenka never so much as glanced back, and I've never seen him since.

A few days after remembering that time sitting with Goenka and our last farewell, a few days after our Wednesday dart-night News meeting, I returned to the Black Sheep Inn. Perhaps I subconsciously hoped to recapture the experience of that other night. But I was there to see a show I'd been told would be right up my alley, mostly, I suspect, because the entertainer had a reputation for being strange. While I waited, a technician slowly did his thing. A short, stout lady holding a hair brush, approached the strands of tinsel hanging from the ceiling in front of the stage. I thought she was going to brush them, but she ran them through her fingers instead and commenced swaying to music playing over the sound system. I would've liked to wait. But, watching that lady for a while was strange enough for one night, and I had my day job to get to in the morning. And, anyway, the moment had passed.

58. Names

Cracks began appearing in the foundation of our business relationship upon only our second meeting. Having chosen a style of engagement ring, and having paid an amount comparable to Nepal's national debt, they had every right to expect me to remember them. I knew I knew them, especially since they grinned like we shared intimate secrets as they came through the shop's doors. For a moment I wondered if we might've had a threesome at some point in time, but reluctantly had to abandon the idea forthwith, though wistfully. Unfortunately, I hadn't the faintest recollection of their names nor where we'd met.

The couple had actually put a down payment on a ring somewhere else until they came to me. And largely due to the force of our connection, because they liked and felt secure with me, they'd changed their idea. After a meeting that was obviously deep and meaningful to them, our shop was given their valuable business; as they walked in just a week later, I absolutely had no idea who they were.

We never really recovered from that low point, especially since I wasn't clear about the job we were doing for them even after some time into the meeting. They phoned the owner next day to complain, he made an appointment to straighten the matter out and, when they came again, I went over to apologise, take them to the owner's office and show them I held no bad feelings. Unfortunately, I had just scoffed down some salted and roasted peanuts. So I walked straight up, gave them my best smile and proceeded to turn beet red, choke, cough, splutter and stagger away. I usually stay away from peanuts.

Forgetting names, however, is a rather frequent problem of mine. It took me all my twenty-three years in India to get a handle on the handles I regularly came in contact with. There was Raju, Rajiv, Rajendre, Rajesh, Roopa, Renu and lots of Rain in summer. Now I have to bend my head around the English names. I really hate to say it, but they all sound the same to me. I'm forever calling Paul Doug, Doug Sir, Larry Lou, Lou Larry, Buck Chuck, and Mike my friend. While working at Ryan's Garage and Famous Folks Company, I was forever calling Ron Bruce, Jacques Jack, Hank Dave, Dave Super, Warren Wayne, Maxine Doreen and Bruce Ron. Of course, there were Trowses all over the place and a flurry of Fleurys of all shapes and sizes, each with a different truck. Some looked and sounded like diesel, but had gas. I'm referring to the trucks. Some looked and sounded like gas, but had diesel. Some looked and sounded like diesel and actually had diesel. Go figure. I had to remember Harvey, Harry, Gaston, Gerry, and Dennis I just watched in awe.

Cecil used to scare the dickens out of me. I could never remember his name, not to mention whether his truck took diesel or gas. He's an intimidating man to someone as unused to the lay of that land as I was. When one night I came back inside the office and told him the amount owing as usual, he muttered something in French as usual which made my legs shake as usual. But I noticed Paul chuckling. So, after he left I asked Paul, whom I called Doug, what Cecil had said; and Paul translated, "You take my money and my heart too." Somehow, I've never forgotten his name since then.

I know the problem doesn't stop with names. After I made a sandwich last night, I put the ingredients back in their place and went to answer the phone. During the ensuing conversation I realised I'd put the cheese in my pocket instead of in the refrigerator. I checked the refrigerator and found the Saran Wrap. I had put my bag of Pierre's life-sustaining sprouts to rot in the cupboard, and as I looked in the cupboard I couldn't remember whether I was putting something in or taking something out.

Without knowing exactly how to take care of the problem of forgetfulness in general, I certainly can suggest several self-help books to aid in one's understanding of the name game. Or I could if I remembered their titles, but I recall only one off-hand. Luckily, it's quite a fine and useful piece of work called Light Of Knowledge. And in chapter two, verse six, it reads; "Every name from straw all the way up to elephant is a name of God."

59. Now That's Garbage

A friend of mine from Winnipeg, who's been living in India nearly as long as I did, came for a visit not too long ago. And I enjoyed spiriting him around to what were for him many unfamiliar places and strange situations. I showed him how not to use his fingers to eat, how not to spit on the side of the road, not to clear his nose onto the sidewalk nor scratch anything private in public. I'm exaggerating, of course, but I did feel like a great and sophisticated man.

My friend's trip not withstanding, just when I believe myself to be fully adjusted to this brave new world, this western civilisation, this free market society, something throws me off my game. One of the little pleasures of my life here has become those New York Fries fries at the Rideau Centre food court. They really stick to your innards. One small size order of fries and I don't have to eat for a week afterward. One medium size order and I walk sideways home and slide my bum along the carpet like a dog with worms. But, they're so good.

Last Tuesday night was a New York Fries night. I ate a small order of fries while watching the people and wondering if I shouldn't have ordered a larger size. Eventually, I made my way to the garbage bin and began to push open the flap when it flipped open all the way on its own. And a voice said, "I'll hold the door open. You throw the garbage in." I jumped back. I'm not particularly proud of it, but my initial thought was that there was someone in there. I realised, nearly instantaneously, that it was a disembodied mechanically generated voice, but the damage had been done. I was out of sorts, totally discombobulated. I looked around to see whether anyone had seen my reaction. Either nobody noticed or they weren't letting on, and I slipped away.

The shock was so still with me next day, however, that I went back again that evening. After a medium-sized order of fries, I made my way to the bin. In fact, I'd brought a pen and paper to jot down the garbage bin's complete repertoire. I wanted the full experience. Of course it was somewhat embarrassing to stand there flagrantly flipping open the flap, but for the sake of research one has to sometimes make some personal sacrifices. First it said, "I'll hold the door open. You throw the garbage in," in a rather sultry voice. Next time it said, "Thank you for not littering. We hope you enjoyed your visit," in the same voice. And then it wouldn't open and a very male voice said, "Please wait. I'm compressing." Apparently, whoever designed the thing felt that it'd be more appropriate if a man were imagined to be doing the work. Finally, while I waited, the same voice, sounding as though he'd just had a big meal, seemed to sort of burp and then said "Ready."

Indians have long since had an innate understanding of recycling. From the good old days when it was known as the 'Golden Sparrow' of the world, through twelve hundred years of foreign rule, India became increasingly poorer; this contributed to a need of the average person to be thrifty. Food was purchased the day it was to be cooked and eaten, water was conserved, paper was re-used in so many ways, food scraps were given to the family cow, and pigs took care of the rest.

Before plastic bags began to litter the landscape, shopkeepers had bags made out of old newspapers, scrapbooks or whatever old paper might've been lying around. I recall just as though it were yesterday the time, while I slurped tea with friends at a local establishment, one of my buddies noticed something odd about his shopping bag. It had obviously been a notebook in a previous incarnation. That wasn't unusual. But, instead of Hindi, the writing on it was English. I noticed that the paper my snack sat on also had English scribbling all over it. And upon closer inspection we came to realise that one of our friends had her old personal diary circulating all around the district.

As much as I appreciate the technology, I really question the need for electronically generated sultry voices to instruct people on the finer points of garbage disposal. It may have been because I'd had New York Fries fries two days in a row, but I left the Rideau Centre that night scratching both my head and my bum. And I didn't feel very sophisticated.

60. Do You Believe In Magic?

I've seen so many miracles in my life that it's difficult to even begin describing them. It's a miracle, for example, that I remained lucid following the late 60s and early 70s. I've seen rain fall without a cloud in the sky, mahatmas walking on red-hot coals, and yogis manifesting themselves in two places at once.

It was a miracle that my friend Steve survived his cancer. The doctors gave him three months to live, but he bargained with them to give him a year. They agreed on six months, but instead Steve went on to become one of the most prominent comedy writers in Los Angeles over the past fifteen years. I've seen a girl younger than three talk more fluently in two languages than I do in one. A Brahma Bull once predicted my future.

In 1995, The Indian Express of Chandigarh reported that idols had been seen to drink milk offerings. The headline read 'Miracle Attracts Thousand to Temples.' The story appeared in the September 22, 1995 edition and said 'Mass hysteria gripped northern India and several other parts of the country as word spread that the idols of the Shiv family were accepting milk offerings, report agencies. Tens of thousands of people thronged temples in a devotional spree to offer milk to marble statues of Lord Shiv, his consort Parvati, son Ganesh and mount Nandi. The reports came from Bombay and Calcutta and even foreign countries, including Nepal, Dubai, U.S.A., and U.K.

'Scientists debunked the event as a case of mass illusion saying that the milk fed in a spoon trickles down in the form of an invisible white film which devotees do not perceive in their excitement. Sceptics scoffed at the idea of idols drinking milk, criticised the enormous wastage of milk and questioned the scientific basis. Thousands of litres of milk was offered at the temples in Delhi alone by this noon, creating an acute shortage of this essential commodity. Milk was being sold at a premium in a number of localities.'

For the next several days, newspapers continued their coverage. 'The mysterious disappearance of milk when offered to the various idols at Punjab, Haryana and Himachal Pradesh continues to baffle the devout and sceptics alike. The phenomenon, reported to have begun in the early hours of the morning on Thursday, has been attracting large, frenzied crowds of the devout who lined up outside temples with polypacks of milk to make offerings to the gods. Police are rushing in force to regulate the crowds and to prevent any untoward happening.'

Unashamedly, I admit that I also tried to feed milk to one of the statues in my home when no one was around. I made a mess in my front room and you may well laugh, but my mind's been pried open. One morning in the late 1970s about twenty-five students, myself among them, sat with our teacher meditating. We were silent except for a fire crackling in the fireplace and the sound of a vehicle passing every now and again up on the road. Unexpectedly, Swamiji spoke, a disembodied voice from out of near total stillness, "Mary's coming down the steps without shoes." A few moments passed before he continued. "Now I feel the dew on the grass as Mary crosses the lawn. I know that because I am her feet and I am the grass." A few moments later the door opened and Mary entered.

I have a friend who tells a story of how she was meditating with her teacher and several other devotees while trying hard to think of a word rhyming with 'mitigate.' She was struggling for some time to properly finish a poem she was writing when, from out of the silence, her teacher said, "litigate." I've heard of a type of medicinal ash, called Vibhooti, inexplicably produced from out of Satya Sai Baba's hands.

It bothers me that I'm becoming more and more predictable to you the longer this column continues. Nevertheless, in conclusion I must write that the greatest miracles I've witnessed, predictably, are the ones I tend to take for granted; the morning sun, stars at night, the river, family, friends, breathing in, breathing out.

To the editor;

As a concerned resident of a proud village, I would like to complain about that fellow, Nathan Vanek, and his column. Since he wrote about the talking garbage bin in the Rideau Centre, I'm forced to join everyone else, especially on a Friday or Saturday night, around that trashcan in Ottawa if I want to see my friends at all. Instead of staying home playing Gin Rummy, watching hockey or getting sloppy drunk, everyone's loitering in town eating New York Fries and hoping for their chance to flip open the lid of that that that thing to hear what its gonna say. It's just not right. If he had wanted to make himself sick, he could've gone to the Jean Burger or eaten a whole basket of fries at Billy's right here at home instead of New York Fries in a foreign centre. But, deep down he's really a foreigner himself, isn't he? I honestly think The News has bigger potatoes to fry and should re-think their decision to print the wandering thoughts of such a person.

Sincerely, Martha (Bonnie's mom).

61. *Some Rain Must Fall*

Walking to my day job one rainy morning last week, as I held an umbrella up high to protect my suit from the rain, I tried to recall a certain verse from out of the famous Bhagawat Gita. I'd have been able to remember it not so many months ago, but I lived in India then. I had to look it up later at home to know that verse 23 from chapter 2, translated from the original Sanskrit reads 'The self is immortal. The self cannot be cut by weapons, burnt by fire, wet by water or embarrassed by wind. It is indestructible. You must realize it.' It was the 'wet by water' part I was relating to most that morning.

When the monsoons swept across the middle ranges of the Himalayas, everyone got wet. Umbrellas were about as useful as sunscreen to a coal miner. The wind would whip them around and turn them inside out, making spindly, cadaverous wrecks of them, like spokes of a bicycle wheel after being run over by the neighbourhood milk truck. During milder rain one might hang an umbrella from the back collar of one's jacket while walking the hillside. Mostly, one just got used to being damp.

By way of contrast, I recall a rather regrettable rainfall on one of my first days back in Canada, as I strolled arm in arm with my cousin Johnny behind my aunt Lucy and uncle Ben down Queen Street in Toronto. It began to drizzle. Initially I hadn't even noticed until my auntie yelled, "Oh, Benny, was that a drop of rain!?" And, before Ben could answer, she hollered, "Oh my God! I felt another one!" Johnny also hadn't noticed. Of course, he wouldn't notice if a bag of cement fell on him. He just lolled his head around grinning as usual and wiping his mouth on my sleeve. But he was born that way. Some of us are born that way and some of us aspire to it. Meanwhile, my aunt and uncle were freaking out. There ensued a feverish discussion about whether it'd be better to attempt a run back to the car or to camp out in a near-by café. Running was out of the question, really. So a street-side delicatessen received our business that morning, though I personally wasn't in the mood to eat anybody's tongue in a sandwich or anyone's liver chopped up and served on a warm plate with garnish. And what was happening outside, in fact, wouldn't even be labelled rainfall back where I'd spent most of my adult life.

Whenever Spring would come to the Himalayas, one could often hear a charming little ditty sung by young and old alike as they skipped through the mustard fields. Loosely translated, it went like this; 'Oh sweet lord of favours. The rain's swallowed the neighbours. Grab little brother by the hand. Run fast to the highland. Never mind your hat and coat. Forget about the family goat,' or something to that effect. There was another that went 'Roses are red. Violets are blue. The neighbour's dead. And so are you. Which is just as well cause I've no intention of going alone.' You could never be sure when the rain would sweep down across the land. But when it did it could rain for days at a time, the river would flood and wash through the town, and houses on the hillside would slip off their foundations or get washed away entirely.

The local newspapers never wanted for headlines. They'd alternate between stories of killer heat waves and homicidal downpours. On April 19th 1995, for example, the Indian Express reported 'Cloudburst Claims Ten More Lives.' And on the 21st, fifty-three more lives were reported lost and yet another one hundred were feared killed in a mudslide just a few days later. Poor people needing fuel for cooking or warmth would stand by the river's edge, during the rains, holding long wooden poles. They'd attach a hook to the end and try to snag wood drifting past. But sometimes, quite often, actually, when the hook latched all of a sudden onto a log or part of a house flying by, the poor sod would get taken by surprise, lurch forward and be swept away.

Meanwhile, life would march on, apple blossoms would dress up the valley while the prescient scent of spring whispered a promise of new beginnings in spite of all indications to the contrary. We'd see the sights and listen to the sounds of creation and destruction both, following them to their one source. And the rain could not make us wet.

62. *Of Mice And Men*

I'm not one of those people who's ready at a moment's notice to demonstrate against hunting. As long as nobody shoots me I figure, hey, 'live and let live.' While still working at Ryan's Famous Garage and Snow-Pushing Company, I noticed a dear dead deer in the back of a very yellow truck that stopped for gas. The very next truck to come in was driven by another, less fortunate, rather frustrated hunter. "Haven't seen a deer all day," he announced. "You seen any deer round bout these parts?" "Come to think of it," I replied, always wanting to be helpful, "I did see one come through just a couple of minutes ago. You can probably catch up if you hurry. It's in the back of a very yellow truck." He looked at me strangely, quickly paid for his gas, and sped off, I presumed, in hot pursuit.

Who hasn't had the urge to kill a mosquito, a housefly, a family member? Okay, I'm not into hunting deer or moose, but mice can really burn my shorts. Many is the time I've felt the urge to strap on a quiver of arrows, slip into battle fatigues and go stalk the wild Indian gerbil. At various times, whilst living in India, I discovered a mouse in my pants (which made two mice), in my shoe, and even in my bed. On my way to Canada customs officials at Heathrow Airport detained me when a nefarious-looking substance was discovered in the bottom of my suitcase. Careful analysis eventually proved the small, dark brown pellets were mouse droppings.

Realising now that Canadian houses have mice too, and having been plagued by one mouse already this season, it seemed only right that I research the indigenous, down-home kind of Wakefield techniques to reduce the mice population. And I've learned several.

For example, there's the cork and bacon grease technique. That's when you take a bottle cork and dunk it in bacon grease, letting the cork soak up the grease, then place it wherever the creatures tend to loiter. Apparently, mice can't resist bacon grease. I don't have that problem myself, but they do. So when they nibble as much of the cork as they can, the mice get so corked up, so to speak, they die. How charming is that?

Next, there's the Coca Cola technique. That's simply when you leave a small bowl of the real thing wherever the critters hang out. Turns out, mice can't burp. Now, there's a tremendous bit of trivia to file away. So after guzzling down a long drink of Coke, the mouse suffers really bad gas and explodes. I'd have to use Pepsi. Since working at Ryan's, where all things Coca-Cola related are taboo, I've been unable to drink the stuff, snort it or sport the logo on a hat. In fact, if I ever try drinking it now, my hand shakes uncontrollably, and I slop it all down my shirt and pants. But Pepsi should work just as well.

My personal favourite is the Portland Cement technique. This one's truly imaginative. What you do is add one quarter Portland Cement to three-quarters flour. Mix it up well and place a bowl of it, with a bowl of water nearby, wherever the mice are likely to go. Apparently mice can't resist the flour, will gobble the stuff right up and then have a refreshing drink of water. Soon afterward, the cement will begin to solidify and basically entomb the mouse from inside. You have to appreciate the person who thought that one up.

I did dispose of the mouse that was bothering me so far this season, though purely by chance. I inadvertently left a half-finished container of New York Fries on the counter. So when I stumbled downstairs in the morning, I found the poor creature belly-up, bloated and with a really bad complexion.

Several years ago, I visited an old palace in the Kangra Valley with my teacher and several friends. During our first days there, we were sipping tea in a large room where a proud elk was mounted on the wall. His antlers were huge, his eyes were wide open, and his whole neck and shoulders protruded from the wall. As bonafide tree-huggers, we all studiously ignored the matter until my teacher turned and said "Nathan, go round and check whether his back end is on the other side."

All options considered, I've decided that in the future I'll employ that type of trap that enables one to catch the mouse alive and re-locate it onto the neighbour's yard. It's really the only humane way to take care of the problem.

63. A Different Easter Story

One lesson I've learned in life is that it's important to keep one's head. Not all truths are in fact true, but that one truly is. A cool head and a steady heart are required for the happy conclusion of any endeavour. Where would I be now if at the first sign of a struggle, following my decision to return to live in Canada, I'd have panicked and run back to India. Well, I'd probably be sitting at the Imperial Hotel sipping cold coffees with ice cream and enjoying year-round leisure and the almost reverential respect of folks over there. But that's not the point.

I'd like to tell you a story about a fellow who really lost his head once, though only once. Murat was an odd character who used to wander all over northern India buck naked, singing and dancing. He was also considered a Sufi Saint, and the people of his day, early seventeenth century, Hindu and Muslim alike, loved him. At the time, the great Moghul ruler, Shah Jahan, was bunged into a house arrest by his eldest son, Aurangzeb, and given poison bit by bit in his food. Then Aurangzeb proceeded to do away with most of his relations, including his young brother, Samrat, who was a devotee of Murat and was Shah Jahan's favourite. It was a dysfunctional family.

Aurangzeb rationalised his duplicity by being an extremist Sunni Muslim hell bent on securing the kingdom for his fundamentalist understanding of the Koran. He eventually demanded that Murat publicly recite the Caliph and, for heaven's sake, put on some clothes. Aurangzeb also wanted Murat to endorse his rule under threat of decapitation. And therein lies the point. The Caliph, loosely translated, goes 'There's but one God, Allah is his name and Mohammed is the prophet of Allah.' Murat declared himself unfit to recite the Caliph saying he's never met either Allah or Mohammed personally. He also stubbornly refused to get dressed or endorse Aurangzeb as the rightful ruler.

Things came to a head, so to speak, one day when Murat was paraded in front of thousands of people through the streets of Old Delhi and up the steps of the Jasmid Masjid, the Friday Mosque. Everyone from devotees to government officials and religious leaders were trying to talk Murat into reciting the Caliph, but to no avail.

The people were crying out for mercy as Aurangzeb offered him one last chance, but Murat just laughed in his face. That didn't go over too well with Aurangzeb. He angrily gave the order, Murat was pushed down onto the blocks, and his head was chopped right off with one blow from the executioner's axe. It rolled down the steps and, to the horror and absolute, freaking amazement of every one of the scores of eye witnesses, Murat got up and went down to retrieve his head. He picked it up laughing hysterically and yelling, "I am God! I am God!" as he climbed back up the steps. Aurangzeb began screaming as Murat approached until Murat fell in a lifeless heap at Aurangzeb's feet. The crowd went completely nuts. They rioted for ten straight days and nights, and Aurangzeb spent the next twenty-five years continuously fighting Hindus, Rajputs and different Muslim sects in a prolonged, desperate attempt to secure his kingdom.

To this day, a monument to Murat stands just near the Jasmid Masjid in the Chandni Chowk district of Old Delhi. Chandni Chowk's a thick market area that I used to frequent several times a year for business purposes and where, by the way, I lost my head on more than one occasion. But each time I'd pass that monument I was reminded of what Murat stood for: unity, the vision of oneness between people of all faiths, freedom of thought, freedom of expression, freedom. And I was always reminded of how important it is to keep ones head even when all around people are losing theirs.

64. Pennies From Heaven

It would've been impossible to figure out exactly when the headache began last Tuesday, much less why. Perhaps I should've left the window open a bit in my bedroom to allow some of that rare Wakefield oxygen in as I slept. I usually do. Perhaps I shouldn't have watched so much television the night before.

In any event, I probably wasn't thinking clearly as I strolled to work through the Byward Market that morning. Since I couldn't see any pebbles, I threw pennies at my friend's office window to get his attention. But my aim was poor. I tossed about four pennies and then a homeless fellow came to scramble after them. It didn't look good. Although he was obviously slightly daft, I didn't quite realize the impression I was creating. The man skidded after the pennies like a Himalayan dancing bear, and people began staring at as though I were a cad. So I walked away. Before turning the corner, however, I saw my friend look down from his office window with a puzzled expression. He and the homeless guy were staring at each other, but my head was throbbing.

As I stepped past the Chateau Laurier Hotel, I thought about a particular meditation retreat in Oregon from about twenty-eight years ago. I'd had a terrible headache at the retreat. Rain fell in torrents all throughout the ten days. It fell loudly and continuously on the roof of the barn where we sat in meditation, and we listened to the storm raging round us until we nearly stopped noticing. Whenever the rain would subside, we'd go outside for a few minutes of meditative walking.

The headache began about six days into the session. It was the type that pounded and surged and made me nauseaated. It felt as though the storm had infiltrated my brain. And, as the hours passed, the headache grew worse as I feebly attempted to observe it with some measure of equanimity.

Eventually, the lady who led the meditation group noticed my discomfort. She was a very psychic lady, although the pained look of despair upon my face and the foam dribbling from my mouth may have given her a clue. She came over as I staggered slowly around the yard and she asked what was happening. I said "This stupid meditation thing's given me a blasted aneurysm, you bitch." Actually, what I said was "I'm experiencing some karmic disturbance in the form of a headache, madam." She suggested I try to follow the pain to its centre, to its very source, get right into it and remember that all forms and phenomena are transitory. She suggested I try to consider that it's not my pain, but merely pain, a true test of my knowledge.

With deep respect, I glanced at the lady and said, "Drugs would be simpler." Actually, I didn't say that. Being way more open-minded, malleable and easily inspired in those days, I re-entered the barn with a renewed sense of hope, though for what I was not sure. I tried to observe every part of the pain as if I were viewing a slide under a microscope. It was not my pain, just pain. I tried hard not to give it power over me. And for a while the headache seemed only to worsen. I knew where it was concentrated and where each of its tentacles stretched.

Finally, I really felt I'd gained a measure of detachment almost without consciously realising it. It became more a mere mass of sensations than a monster. It was a toothless tiger, powerless. And then, all of a sudden, it burst like a dam. A tidal wave of tingling heat washed through my whole body. As terrible as the pain had been, that pleasurable was the sensation of heat sweeping down to the tips of my toes and back again. At first, I revelled in it. I was momentarily consumed by some kind of ecstasy, until I had a slightly sobering realisation. I realised that there was no essential difference between the pains I'd been observing or the pleasure it changed into. They were not only connected. They were, in fact, one. And I found myself looking at the world just a little differently after that.

Meanwhile, by that time I was on Sparks Street. So I stepped back into the moment, greeted my co-workers and began the daily routine, though not before taking one extra-strength Tylenol with a cup of coffee, no sugar.

65. God's Design

It'd be incredibly unprofessional as well as insensitive of me to write about people or situations that happen at my place of employment, the jewellery store on Sparks street. It'd also be just plain bad karma. The ramifications of doing so could be far-reaching, and I might well have to live with those consequences for the rest of my life.

On the other hand, if they wanted real professionalism they should've hired a lawyer. So a lady came into the jewellery shop, in which I hang in Ottawa, with the idea of having a piece of jewellery created. And, while I'm not much of a designer, I did my best to facilitate matters. I'm really good at washing windshields, administering distemper shots to puppies, and playing basketball against people under five-and-a-half feet in height, but jewellery design's just not my thing.

The lady talked quite slowly, though she appeared normal in most other respects. Every now and again, however, she'd blurt out "How are you?," apparently to no one in particular. And each time she asked, I'd say I was fine. The third time, not being the sharpest tool in the shed myself, I was about to answer her yet again, but she told me not to bother. Then she proceeded to laugh like a hyena.

Anyone, by the way, who has ever lived in the middle reaches of the Himalayas knows exactly where that saying, 'laughed like a hyena,' comes from. On any given evening there, one can hear the high-pitched, shrill cry of the creatures communicating with one another, as the hair on the back of your neck stands on end. Many's the dark night I've skulked along the mountain paths, feeling my way step by step, and shuddered involuntarily when the hyena's cry would tear through the silence. And that's exactly how I felt sitting across from that lady that day. I soon realised she was also prone to rather sudden and severe mood swings.

We eventually finished our discussion, and I began to type the details, of the ring to be made, into a computer. Neither of us was speaking. I'm not sure what came over me, but I blurted out, "How are you?" to no one in particular. The lady positively jumped back and yelped "I'm fine! I'm fine! Thanks for asking!" Then she told me about her schizophrenia, her hospitalisation, even the effects of her medication. Apparently, no one ever asks her. She also told me about her fight with bouts of severe paranoia, which I'm not helping by reporting all this to the people of the Gatineau Hills. Can you imagine if, just by chance, she happens to leaf through a charming little local paper called 'The Low Down To Hull and Back News' on a day trip to Wakefield while lapping up a Slurpy at the general store? That would set her back a few months.

In the end, after all was said and done, the lady shook my hand and said, "God bless you." As I expressed my thanks she said "I mean your God." So I said, "You're God too." Then she said, "No. I mean your God." Of course I responded by insisting that she was also God. "No," she hollered angrily, "I mean, may Your God bless you." "I hope so," was all I said then she laughed like a hyena.

A few short days later, as I returned from a lunch-break, I saw the same lady near the back of the shop. She'd cropped off all her hair, and I could see the hospital tag around her wrist. She was yelling at the owner of the shop because she had been under the impression her ring would be made within a few short days. I tried to back out through the doors but the owner, my employer, called my name. He looked rather like a man who was about to laugh like a Hyena, so, while my co-workers snickered, I had to face the music.

We rode an emotional rollercoaster together, she and I, for the next while until a resolution was agreed upon, I hope. Then she grinned at me from across the desk with sad, hollow eyes. "I have no idea why I've become like this," she said. "Only, I truly believe we're all children of God." She took my hand. "So God bless you," she said sincerely. And I said, "May your God bless you too."

66. *You Are What You Eat*

My buddy, Dan, and I began driving home around midnight. We'd been camping near Huntsville when a bee stung him. Being allergic to bee stings, Dan's face blew up like a balloon and, aside from me not wanting to share a tent with someone resembling Quasimodo, we thought we should get him to a doctor. Chugging along in my little Volkswagen Beetle during the darkest part of the night in northern Ontario, all of a sudden we saw the unmistakable flashing lights and siren of an RCMP cruiser.

It was impossible for us to have been speeding. My old car just couldn't get it up, so to speak. And we hadn't robbed anybody. It could only be one thing ... a drug bust!

We hadn't smoked any spliffs since leaving our campsite. Our attention was more on Dan's increasingly distorted facial bone structure than on recreational drugs, but of course we did have rather substantial nuggets of hashish in each of our pockets. The cops were streaking up behind us like bounding cheetahs, the lights were pulsating in through the small rear window, and the siren was piercing our eardrums, rattling our brains. We panicked. As they climbed right up our tails, Dan and I began eating the stuff like it was Reese's Pieces.

Meanwhile, we pulled over onto the shoulder of the highway and stopped. In a few moments a flashlight blinded me and the officer said, "Are you aware, sir, that one of your tail-lights is burnt out?" I was suitably shocked and dismayed by that news and reassured the officer of my intention to remedy the situation as soon as the first shards of sunlight shone through at dawn. The other constable, meanwhile, strutted up to the passenger side, pointed his big black flashlight, quite obviously compensating for his lack of penile girth, into Dan's face and jumped back with a semi-stifled yelp. They seemed somehow satisfied then with my promise and allowed us to carry on. In fact, they seemed fairly well pleased to see the back of us.

Of course we were overjoyed to be free. We even chortled on about how we'd duped Canada's national police force. But, we also had a niggling feeling we'd made a slight mistake. When we began laughing over the matter like it was the single funniest happening of our entire lives, we knew we were tripping. When I swerved to miss a herd of Wildebeests, which we both saw as clearly as day crossing the highway, we had no more doubt. Eventually, we had to stop. We sat in the car absolutely frozen in time, except for whatever thoughts and images paraded through our minds, for the next many hours. And when we finally resumed the journey, we were both still tripping heavily; but Dan's face was nearly back to normal.

That was about thirty years ago. I stopped smoking or doing any drugs not long afterward. Then my girlfriend left me. Then I became a Vipassana Buddhist monk in California. Then I left for India. I resisted temptation all through Greece, Turkey and Afghanistan. And one of the first things my teacher said, upon our very first meeting in India, was that I had to stay away from drugs of any sort in order to repair the damage I'd done to my nervous system. And he made me promise that, no matter if I returned to the Vipassana monastery, stayed with him, or went anywhere else in the world, I would never even smoke one joint. And so I didn't, well, except for once.

About seven years later I had one quick drag off a reefer of pot, just to be sociable, with a few people. It was a tiny, skinny joint which turned out to be rather more powerful than I'd anticipated, the net result being that I became completely and utterly consumed with paranoia. While everyone else joked and laughed, I went totally catatonic.

After eventually finding my way home, I sat still for a long time on my bed until I felt an irresistible urge to go see my teacher. So I sneaked into the main hall where he was giving a discourse to about two hundred people. I just sat there in my paranoid state of mind well hidden behind the crowd listening until, from out of nowhere, my teacher said, "Oh, look how blessed Nathan is today!" And two hundred people turned around to look at me.

67. Time After Time

There was an odd little fellow who used to do odd little jobs around my odd little house in India. He had less than stellar personal hygiene and didn't do such great work but he'd always just been there, part of the family as it were. His name was, and I presume still is, Balayati Ram. He had a weakness for the local liquor, which was known to cause blindness. But Balayati was made of different stuff. His eyes remained just fine. Unfortunately, he went nearly deaf instead. And although I'd given him a western raincoat, during the monsoons he used to proudly sport a full-length coat made of clear plastic bubble-paper instead. The point is, I could've sworn I saw him on Sparks Street one evening last week.

I'm feeling pretty good about the choices I've made in life. Of course, it might just be the veggie burger I had this afternoon at Chez Eric's. Lord knows it's not always easy to live with the choices one makes, but really one has little choice. It's even harder to find a really fine veggie-burger. Nevertheless, when you start seeing your former hired-help thousands of miles away, a man who's never even been to the neighbouring valley, a man who changes his clothes only on special occasions, one has to sit back on one's haunches and reflect a little. Have I, in fact, adjusted or have I just had a great lunch? Why do I have to figure out where I am, for a moment or two, some mornings upon awaking?

In the village where I lived in India there was another odd little man who often came a knocking at my door, badgering me to do odd little charitable works which would, incidentally, directly benefit him. Looking like Howdy Doody with Dumbo ears, he prided himself on his inhumanly early morning walks, fully suited up, after which he'd often bang down my door like a drill sergeant. His name was, and I presume still is, Mr Naval Thakur, pronounced Tucker.

Once one got to know him, certain possible rhyming nicknames would pop into one's mind involuntarily. I was on a Greyhound Bus to Hawksbury a few weeks ago, having left my car in Ottawa, when it took me nearly thirty minutes of severe if familiar discomfort to realize there was a toilet at the back. Indian buses don't have toilets. The thing is, I could've sworn I saw Mr Naval Thakur sitting three-quarters of the way back on that bus.

The oddest little character of all was a guy who used to walk around my village in India always three sheets to the wind, so to speak. He wasn't drunk. He was just odd. He'd sleep on the shoulder of the road right in front of my house, backside bared for all the world to see. It was always pointed at the road in such a way that every vehicle heading north would catch the full faecal fracture full on in their headlights. During the days he'd stand around arguing alone, jabbing the air with one hand while holding up what was left of his trousers with the other. The point is, although I've never seen him over here, I often see a fellow on Rideau Street who may be his brother.

I'm sure I met Sam, the black dog who hangs around the Radisson Building, not long before leaving India. He doesn't seem to remember. I keep seeing people from there over here and folks here I swear I've known over there, or at least known somewhere before. I awake in the dead of night, sweating, with the distinct feeling I'm neither here nor there. But that's another matter. The point is, I'm suspicious. I'm far from certain, but I suspect we've all been here before.

68. *The Never-Ending Story*

There was a time in the late eighties when Swamiji decided to go for early morning walks down the one road through the valley. That time of day was the only really peaceful time on the road and the only really cool time in the valley. Swamiji walking, of course, meant that at least fifty or so people would go along, crowding in as close as possible to hear, perhaps even participate in, what he'd be talking about.

Being one of the least aggressive students, however, meant that I'd perpetually find myself shuffling along from somewhere near the middle of the herd, walking on the heels of people ahead, getting shoved from side to side. One morning, while treading along, I began to bleat like a sheep. I thought I was being rather clever, but the whole crowd turned around to glare at me. In fact, the only one laughing was Swamiji. He found my bleating immensely funny and had me walk beside him for the rest of the morning.

Needless to say, that story brings me to the tragic events of the past few weeks in Walkerton, not to speak of the safety of swimming in the rivers and lakes these days. The contaminated water in Walkerton was not unlike countless outbreaks of water-born diseases that occur in India on a fairly regular basis. In fact, the same happening would hardly raise eyebrows in the country. Mexico's Montezuma's Revenge has its Indian equivalent in what's known as Delhi Belly which, while obviously less severe than the deadly E-Coli bacteria, can still be awfully uncomfortable. I know. I've had both Monty's Revenge and Delhi Belly. In fact, my system is so adapted to poor water by now that Walkerton could probably hire me as a taste tester.

Where I lived in India, no rational human being would drink water from the taps. Those who survived such a practice would surely produce mutant babies with extra appendages. Much like the good folks of Wakefield, we'd carry out jugs each evening to the local temple, where an ever-running flow from an underground spring supplied us with drinking and cooking water. Friends would stroll along while discussing local politics, often having to be pulled apart by more friends when arguments broke out over the issues. Local boys would compliment the girls' jugs as they walked by. Cadaverous looking local canine creatures would skip in and out of the line, playing and fighting with each other.

I heard an interesting conversation recently between a local boy and a lady cottager, both collecting water from the spring at Valley drive. I say the fellow was a boy, though he could probably have ploughed his back forty alone hitched up to a plough. The lady was probably from a city somewhere, small, with frilly little dress, waiting to fill up while remarking upon the apparent wastage of water. She felt we needed a faucet.

The boy smiled good-naturedly up at her and said it's not a waste because the water runs from the spring to the river. The lady insisted that not being able to turn off the water was a tremendous waste of the good stuff. So the boy, by then slightly peeved, said, "How can it be a waste when the water is a never-ending flow from the underground spring to the Gatineau river, to the Ottawa river and on to the ocean, from the ocean to clouds, to rain and back to the spring? It's a continuous cycle." Even still, even after that, the stubborn lady would not back down. The boy just shrugged, looked at me as if to say, 'She's your problem now,' and walked away with his supply of the good stuff to his truck. Personally, I thought he'd spoken a profound truth, an allegory of life itself. I wanted to follow and sit at his feet for further teaching.

Every early morning, during our walks with Swamiji, we'd pass by that temple where the fresh spring water gushed continuously out of a pipe. I remember, as if it were yesterday, watching the Babas, those wandering mendicants and holy sadhus, performing their morning prayers, thanking the gods for the precious water. Filtration systems changed a lot in India where I lived. But, long after we could more safely drink the tap water, even up to today, many people still stroll with their jugs in the evening to the temple, more as a testimonial to the importance water plays in their lives than out of any need.

69. *Friend Finder*

Leave me alone for a few days and I start surfing the Internet. Somebody should really tie one of my back feet to a peg in the yard. Being on the first vacation from my day job since what feels like about 1937, I've been so on-line that it's strange to recall that I lived most of my adult life in India, the land of electrical wires hanging off mail boxes and telephone lines wrapped around low branches.

Having caught up on my e-mailing and the basketball news, and having played chess with several faceless Internet players around the world, I came across a strange site called the 'Adult Friend Finders.' And the folks who've posted personal advertisements on it are very friendly indeed. In fact, the word 'friend' could be considered somewhat of an understatement.

The most adult entertainment one might come across in India would be the viewing of ancient carvings of curvaceous ladies and their well-hung men on temples like Kajuarahao, or leafing through books with erotic paintings from the Kama Sutra. The Kama Sutra shows various positions for love-play, everything from the missionary position to something that looks like a naked man performing the Heimlich manoeuvre from behind a naked lady.

Without intending to minimise their entertainment value, after viewing the temples and the Kama Sutra one is at a loss to know what to do. It's not as if one ever actually gets to try out those positions. And as modest as Indian society still is, I'm not trying to say there's no sex. You don't produce a billion people by being ignorant about it.

Before actually searching for a new friend on the Adult Friend Finders site, you have to sign in and choose certain options. For example you have to decide where you'd like your new friend to be found, his or her age, the range being between eighteen and about ninety-five, and what type of friendship you're looking for. You have to decide whether you'd like to find a lady or a man or a person simply dressed like a lady or a man. Do you want one friend or groups of friends? Would you like to just watch or actually join in?

The only category I couldn't quite comprehend involved the question of whether you're interested in water-sports. After first understanding, and then deciding, whether you're into groups, miscellaneous fetishes, bondage, masochism, and/or domination, all of a sudden you're asked if you're into water sports. I used to be a fairly good water-skier in my day, but I suspected that wasn't the right final answer. But, please, don't nobody tell me.

There were sixteen thousand, five-hundred and sixty-three listings in Quebec, though only four-hundred and eighty-two of them were women seeking men. The rest were women seeking women, men seeking men, women seeking couples, men seeking groups, women seeking German Shepherds or men seeking Jersey cows. There was every type of assumed name from Queen Zulu to Angel Zombie, from Happy Ming Ming to Wilted Lilly. It's a far cry from the days when names like Sita and Lakshmi seemed exotic to me.

After cruising through the personal ads of several provinces and a few states, I became morally outraged. However, I thought that, before signing off, I'd just take one look at who was advertising for a new friend in Ontario. And there was something about one of the photos, of a lady calling herself 'Mama,' that I found somewhat disquieting. The photos are tiny until one clicks on them to see them enlarged. When I did, I saw a photo of 'Mama' was actually mama! I mean, she was my mama! 'Eighty-plus playmate looking for a real man,' she wrote as a heading. Which presumably meant dada wasn't a real man. OK she wasn't really my mama, but she must've been somebody's.

If I wanna buy a pair of hiking boots from the LLBean web-site, I might take the chance of ordering them before sticking my big feet in to see whether it's a nice fit. I'm not sure the same holds true in the case of ordering a new friend. On the other hand, in India you mostly don't get to see your new friend's face until the wedding ceremony. I was recently introduced to my new friend by mutual friends in Ottawa, which I think is a nice way. The only problem is she sheds a lot and hasn't quite got the hang of the litter box yet.

70. Freedom's Heart

Walking along Sparks Street in my usual afternoon lunch-break stupor, I stumbled across an elephant and became instantly disoriented. Normally by that time of the workaday, I shuffle forward hunched, leaning into the wind, though there be no wind, trying desperately to take in some oxygen.

Some colour had returned to my cheeks, circulation had begun to flow again and I was beginning to straighten up when I saw the large, grey pachyderm. The superimposition of such a proud symbol of the east onto this western capital region's famous outside shopping mall knocked the wind right out of me again. The colour drained from my cheeks, and the left side of my face involuntarily began trembling.

Although I haven't been living in this part of the jungle long, if there were elephants I might've at least spotted one roaming around somewhere, sometime. I had no idea. A man, striding along beside the beast, guided him or her with a stick; and a boy followed behind with a garbage bag and a shovel. Both gentlemen, as well as the elephant, wore red shirts with the words, 'You Ain't Seen Big Yet,' or something to that effect. I had no idea what they were advertising, but my attention had drifted to the boy bringing up the rear, so to speak.

The fellow couldn't have been more than twenty or so, perhaps scooping his way through college, and he shot me a toothy smile. "It's a living," he said with a shrug and a thinly veiled embarrassment. "Must be kinda strange, though," I responded with a friendly candour. Predictably, just as the boy began to get defensive, the elephant opened up his gates to let the calves out, if you catch my drift, and a great, heaping, steaming pile landed on the boy's running shoes. Hard to really defend your choice of summer jobs after that.

Meanwhile, a nubile young girl was running round in circles, gesticulating wildly, imploring the crowd to stop watching because it was so cruel. She was flushed, waving her arms in front of the elephant and shouting for everyone to move along. "Stop this travesty! Stop this travesty!" she hollered. And as much as I may have agreed, my feet seemed glued to the sidewalk.

I've seen enough elephants. I was more interested in the boy scooping and the girl ranting on about the inhumane treatment of animals. The more the girl insisted I not watch, the harder it was to tear myself away. She was creating quite a scene. She'd obviously been the victim of cruelty herself, as evidenced by all the rings and studs in her face- several in her ears, across her eyebrows, her lip, her tongue, and one horrific ring through her nose. She may have been led about by a rope attached to that nose-ring like so many water buffalo, Himalayan brown bears and Brahma bulls I've seen. Certainly, we could all understand her feelings, but the elephant seemed to be having his or her own fun, and I had to get back to the shop. My time was up.

Needless to say, there's nothing quite like viewing God's own creatures in their natural habitat. I've seen a mountain lion leading her cubs along the side of a hill and a grizzly bear standing in an icy stream. I've watched wild horses, jackals, mongoose, baboons and exotic dancers do their thing. But the most mystical wild animal I've seen by far was a snow leopard bounding right by me along the jungle's edge in the Kangra Valley. I still have dreams about that sight.

On the other hand- and I don't wish that girl to ever see similar sights, given her fine sensibilities- I've spotted monkeys chained to the sides of speeding trucks, cobras drugged up and languishing in baskets. I've seen cows forever tethered on such short lines that they were not able to raise their heads. And I've seen ladies, for that matter, covered from the tops of their heads down to their toes in black robes for their whole lives.

So, as I cleaned the sign in front of our shop later that same afternoon, I reflected upon all I'd seen and heard. I couldn't help chuckling at the memory of that silly boy having to shovel up all the elephant's stuff. And, as I wiped up the last of the pigeon droppings from the sign, I made a mental note to never condone the enslavement of elephants or any creature meant to roam God's green earth in freedom.

71. The Pitter-Patter of Litter Feet

My new roommate's name is Morris2. Morris2 is a cat, but I certainly wouldn't tell him that. He's quite convinced he's a person, though he eats like a horse. I like to think I saved him from a life of crime on the streets of Ottawa by offering him a room in my house for some time. But, after hardly a few weeks you'd think he owned the place.

One lady I know in Toronto talks to her cats as if they're people, and I always made fun of her for that. Now, every morning as I'm leaving for work, I find myself asking Morris2 just to do the dishes or maybe the laundry but, you know, every evening I see that nothing's been done. I find myself discussing sports and politics with him and, although he's lazy, he actually does have some pretty good ideas.

I haven't had a lot of success with cats. The last time I had a cat was years ago in India. They're mostly wild there, but some kids brought an abandoned kitten to me. Morris1 had been separated too early from mommy, was quite ill, and wouldn't eat a thing. He was wasting away quickly. I put bowls of milk, bread, cheese, eggs in front of him. Nothing worked until I went to the market, brought home a can of Tuna, and gave him a taste. The little fellow went absolutely rangy, so I gave him a bit more. He gobbled it up as though there was no tomorrow. And, as it happened, there was no tomorrow. It was so great to see him eating that I gave him the whole damn tin. Morris1 shat his brains out and died later that same day. I realised, rather belatedly, that I should've started him off a tad more slowly, and I resolved to be more careful next time, which is now.

The folks in Ottawa, who asked if I'd take in Morris2, assured me that this was a male. It really didn't matter to me what gender he or she was. It wasn't as if I'd eventually have to come up with a dowry to get her married off. The matter only came up later on when a friend was visiting from India. Although she's written the quintessential top-selling Hindi grammar book used at Cambridge and other schools, Chaytna is most famous for having one of the portliest dogs in all of northern India. She just loves feeding all the hungry creatures around, and Lord knows I've been one of them.

One day I noticed that Morris2 seemed to be spreading out rather rapidly. I accused Chaytna of making my cat fat, but she insisted that Morris2 wasn't fat but pregnant. It was hard to know how to react to that idea. Biology wasn't my strong suit, but something seemed off. Chaytna, however, did an examination and confidently declared that Morris2 was indeed a Mary, with a bun in the oven. And while not overjoyed, at least I was reassured the world was working in the way I've always understood it was supposed to.

Nevertheless, that changed everything. Although I wouldn't accept responsibility for Mary's condition, I promised to raise her kids as my own. I made a nice bed for her out of large boxes, blankets and pillows. And I awaited delivery. Two days afterward, Chaytna left for parts unknown, and Mary and I settled in to watch a basketball game on television. I figured it'd be cool to lie together on the sofa, she being a she and pregnant and all. Only, during one of the time-outs, Mary climbed up and started humping my left leg. It really doesn't matter whether it was my left or right leg. I cried foul and pushed her off onto the floor. And while I may not be the sharpest tool in the shed, the significance of the moment was not lost on me.

I can't even remember the last time anybody tried to hump my leg, but I'm pretty darn sure it wouldn't have been a female. So I got up and rolled Mary over to take my own good look for the very first time; there, standing tall and proud in plain sight and living colour, was clear evidence of his manhood. I knew it was an exciting basketball game, but that was ridiculous. Well that changed everything, again. I put Morris2 on a diet right away and went upstairs to change my pants. The long and short of it is, I haven't seen a mouse since Morris2 moved in. He took care of that problem. But, now I have a cat. And, so far as I can recall, no mouse has ever tried to hump my leg.

72. I Think Therefore I'm Not

There must be an Albert on Albert Street There must be a spark on Sparks Street, somewhere. There's lots of banks on Bank Street, one or more queens on Queen Street, I'm sure. There must be Plunketts on Ch. Plunkett, Trowses or Trowsi on Ch. Trowse. There must be wolves up at Ch. Du Lac des Loups, foxes running round Ch. Fox Run and the river flows alongside Riverside Drive. There's a market certainly in the Byward Market, and for sure there are several black sheep hanging out at that Inn of the same name. It's a shame there's no street called 'Truth.'

Truth is a funny old thing. Pete Seeger, whom I bumped into once in New Delhi, of all the unlikely places to meet one's childhood folk-hero, said Truth is like a rabbit in a briar patch. You rarely get a firm hold of it. You can only point and say it's in there somewhere. There's an old Dakota tribal saying that when you find yourself riding a dead horse, you can try a bigger whip, but really it's best to dismount. The Dakota thing doesn't exactly go with the point I'm trying to make, but I just kinda like it.

In India, there's a word for that which is untrue. 'Maya' is that which appears true and real, but which turns out to be quite untrue and unreal, like seeing a stick in the darkness and thinking it's a deadly snake. Aware of the stick and snake analogy, I've learned that things are not always what they seem. And it's a fatal flaw in anyone to totally believe what he/she thinks is always right or the only truth. And if anyone disagrees with me they can roast in Haiti for all I care.

Let me offer an example of what I mean. One late night, a while back, fresh from my bath and having shaken off all excess water, I slithered over to close the living-room window. There was a breeze, and I was chilled. The window, however, being a rather warped, antiquated affair, was sticking; and no matter how hard I tried, it just wouldn't budge. I eventually had to balance myself up on the sofa, under the hanging lamp, and pound the bejesus out of the frame to loosen it, trying to wrench it free. As luck would have it, a neighbour was jogging by just then. It would've looked to all the world as though I was knocking on the window to get his attention, and unfortunately I was buck naked at the time. There I was, standing under the glare of the lamp, banging on the window, and so it follows that what Mr Neighbour must've concluded, as he turned to wave, a look of horror spreading across his features, just wasn't right. He had no business jogging at that time of night anyway.

Walking through the Clarica building in Ottawa recently, heading for an escalator, I saw the escalator and what I thought was a second one off to the side in an adjoining room. I went for the escalator off to the side and smacked into a funny-looking fellow with big ears coming toward me. I begged his pardon and moved to allow him to pass, but so did he. I realised, pretty much simultaneously, that I'd bumped into my own reflection in a mirrored wall … and apologised. It all happened quickly, as life tends to go in the city, so I looked around to see if anyone had been watching. Of course no one was, and I scurried away.

The ancient sages referred to this world as 'Maya', a magical illusory show. A wise man I knew in India used to say, "If you haven't any spare change, just give me a smile." Oh, excuse me. That was Dave, the fellow who wears the red and white top hat on the corner of Queen and Bank Street. The wise man I knew in India used to say, "Truth is that which makes you and the people around you happy."

73. *Love A Good Parade, or Bigger Is Not Better*

For some reason, I had the impression that the Wakefield Canada Day parade began at nine in the morning. It seemed an ungodly hour for a parade, and apparently the whole village felt the same since I was the only jerk walking up and down Riverside Drive wondering where everyone was. Eventually, I stumbled back home only to learn, purely by chance along the way, that it was scheduled for twelve.

It was, of course, well worth the wait, what with our own beloved village poet leading the procession as the fire truck sounded its siren and clanged its bell. There were costumes, cub scouts, brownies, candies, antique trucks, muscle cars and golden retrievers all over the place. I met a couple from Watertown who were pouring over the parade's route map while trying to control several kids. Of course I suggested they keep their heads up but, although I've seen lots of parades, love a good parade, am almost a parade aficionado, I'm bound to use the Wakefield Canada Day parade as a point of reference from now on.

In India, there's a day set aside each year for fireworks. As I awaited the Wakefield fireworks later that evening, I recalled times long passed when Diwali, the Indian festival of lights, was all about little clarified butter lamps on doorsteps and in windows. Later on it 'evolved' into a day of cherry bombs. My friend John, a shell-shocked Vietnam War veteran type, inevitably ended up under a table at some point during the day. We'd be sipping tea at a café when someone would light off a cracker, sending poor John hurtling for cover. And he wouldn't come back up until I assured him the Cong had retreated back into the jungle.

In India, there were copious fireworks injuries, even tragedies and I hardly participated in the festivities, although I did light a rocket off once beside my house on the hillside. That being my first time, wouldn't you know it, the rocket exploded right as I lit the thing. I staggered around the hillside shaking my burnt fingers and shouting expletives that people must've heard several villages away.

In India, boys used to derive great pleasure out of shooting rockets down the street instead of up into the air. You'd be walking along when, all of a sudden, you'd find yourself dodging projectiles headed straight for you. During one Diwali, after dark and during the same time when the road turned into a war zone, a rocket swooshed down, weaving from side to side and, like one of those smart missiles, headed purposefully straight in through the front door of a shop full of fireworks. It exploded inside the place and soon the fit hit the shan, as it were. In other words, all hell broke loose.

The deafening noise galvanised people of the area into action. The neighbouring houses were emptied of cows, televisions and, since there was still time, children and old people as the area became Beirut-esque, Kosovo-like, World War Two-ish. As I participated in the human chain, handing bucket after bucket of sand forward to throw onto the fire, I heard someone yell that there was a gas tank inside. I tore up the street like a bounding cheetah, slinking back like a jackal after hearing that the tank had been empty.

As the Wakefield Canada Day fireworks commenced, the whole crowd 'oohed' and aahed' even before the first display burst with colour or shattered the night with its bang, The thing was still on its way up as folks began making strange noises of appreciation. I've seen a few major fireworks displays over the years but, on the grounds of the Wakefield community centre that night, it didn't seem to be about bigger or better. The focus seemed as much on community magic as on the show. Of course, I could be wrong. Maybe bigger is better, though, God, I hope not.

If you were to ask people in major cities around the world what would make them happier, you'd get answers like a new car, a bigger house, a raise in pay, a face-lift, hair transplant. Hardly anyone would say Canada Day in Wakefield. Still, I rather enjoy applauding a parade that applauds back. And how can you help but get happy being part of a crowd that's appreciative before a match ever touches its first wick.

74. The Laughing Buddha

In the first year of living in Canada, since my traumatic initiation into the world of bankcards and instant cash machines, I studiously avoided 'plastic.' But, then Tony the Tiger sent me a card for Esso with a chance to win a trip to California, a Sport Utility Vehicle or a bottle of windshield washer fluid. The I.G.A. offered me a card. I got a card from The Bay, Eaton's even after it went belly-up, bankcards and green hospital cards. Eventually I had cards coming out my yazoo. I couldn't even remember what some of them were for, and I could often hear the distant sound of Buddha laughing at my folly.

Recently I was advised to consolidate most of my cards into one which has an air miles points system. The fellow who advised me, unfortunately, has a debt load so large he applied for help from the World Bank, a fact that I admit did give me a moment's pause. That moment, however, passed, and so now I keep just the one card with which I carry out my transactions. The points go toward flights on Air Canada and all connector airlines such as Yak Air, Nippon, VARIG, whatever the heck that is, and Mexicana Air. So you can imagine how happy I am now, and it's a heck of a lot easier on the yazoo.

I received the new card just before a short trek to Toronto and was quite eager to buy, buy, buy so I could collect, collect, collect air mile points for a visit to India. Halfway, however, I stopped at Tim's for a coffee, but the card wouldn't work in the bank machine. It didn't work in the phone. I couldn't even buy a honey-dipped donut with the blasted thing. I coasted on fumes to a stop in front of my parents' apartment, cranky, parched and hungry with blood sugar level somewhere down around my ankles. I called the card company and, suffice it to say, they fixed their mistake and sent me out a new card.

The first thing I noticed upon eventually receiving the initial credit card bill was, 'YOUR ACCOUNT IS NOT UP TO DATE AND THE ACCU-MULATED MILES OF 3385, INCLUDING 2500 WELCOME BONUS POINTS, HAVE NOT BEEN AWARDED.' I really didn't give a rat's tail how many points they WEREN'T awarding me, bonus or otherwise. I just would've preferred not to be treated as though I'd committed a major fraud on the state. It put me right off my broccoli. As the mayor of Hiroshima said during dinner, "What the fork was that?" I'm a fellow so filled with fear and loathing of debts that I pay bills practically the minute after they fall into my mailbox. If I'm expecting a substantial one, I'll even go wait for the ever-dependable Mr George Berthiaume at the Alpengrus mail boxes.

Needless to say, they straightened their mistake, again, and I've calcu-lated that within two years of constantly waving that plastic magic wand I'll have enough air mile points for a flight to Sarnia. Coincidentally, I acci-dentally typed 'want' at first instead of 'wand.' The Buddha said that being free of desires is the key to peace of mind that, of course, is not a concept I'm the least interested in entertaining at the moment. In fact, I wish he'd stop following me and go back to his Bodhi tree where he may find someone who cares.

It's a far cry from the way I used to do my banking in India during 'the early days.' A representative of the State Bank of India would come twice a week and sit under a tree with a green, tin box and a ledger. A second, larger fellow, would sit cross-legged behind with an old double-barrelled shot gun resting on his knees. That's kinda like, not wanting to make too fine a point, what I hear La Caisse Populaire does these days somewhere in Le Manoir Wakefield.

I'm obviously excited about a trip to wherever Yak Air goes. I haven't any idea where that might be, although I have a feeling I'd better pack a sweater. But, even though I may fly all over this wide, wild world on my points, I also have a feeling I'll be looking over my shoulder to see if Mr Buddha's following, laughing, pointing out how I've forgotten that happi-ness comes from within. He's a card.

75. Evil Dogs, Part One

My cat Morris and I were flipping though the Ottawa Sun together last Friday night when we came across a rather interesting article. I was doing the flipping because he rips the pages with his claws. From Mohanpur, India, the headline read; 'Girl Marries stray Pooch.' 'A fourteen-year old Indian girl,' the story began, 'has married a dog in a traditional Hindu service. The bizarre ceremony was prompted by an astrologer who told the girl's father the ceremony would transfer the evil effects of the planet Saturn from the girl to the dog.'

My initial reaction was one of shocked disbelief. I mean, that's no reason to get married. What about love? So I read on, trying to understand. 'The girl, Anju, had suffered several illnesses, had fallen in ponds, fractured bones and burnt her hand in the kitchen, said the father. Anju and the dog, whose name was Bullet, were married with Hindu priests chanting hymns in front of one-hundred and fifty guests in a village sixty kilometres north of Calcutta. Police said they were aware of the ceremony, but not bothered by it.'

A photo accompanied the article and, while I admit they made a cute couple, I couldn't help shaking my head in dismay. Morris, of course, seemed quite alright with the whole affair, kept grinning stupidly up at me all evening and purring in a most unsettling fashion. I suppose, if you look at it from the pooch's point of view, the arrangement doesn't seem half bad. Hard to go back to the kennel after that. And obviously, if Anju's luck didn't change, it appears her time could be counted in doggie years. But, what if the pundits were correct in their assertion that some evil could actually be transferred to Bullet? Anju might wanna be fairly careful about that before crawling into bed on her honeymoon night. I've seen my share of evil dogs, I can tell you, and it's often not been very pretty.

Years ago in India, for example, I had to deal with a nasty rabid dog.

Several friends had travelled in a line of taxis up to the higher reaches of the Himalayas, above the clouds, to a place called Rohtang Pass. We walked through snow, sat on rocks and drank hot tea by a fire inside a rough, wooden tea stall before heading back. How could Amy have known that a slobbering, mad, evil dog would jump out at her just as she came from her taxi? The large, brown and black mutt bit her leg repeatedly, ferociously, before bounding off into the dark night. Amy was crying, screaming, as we carried her home.

The doctor came running. And as he tended Amy, Dr Gaurav explained to us the importance of finding out if the dog was indeed rabid. So three different groups immediately went off in search of the animal. My buddy Krishn Kaant and I jumped into a van and cruised the area. We learned along the way that six local people had ended up in the hospital because of that same creature, one or two in such serious condition that their very life was in question.

Just before eleven at night, we thought we might have spotted the dog. It was weaving back and forth down the road, and as we came alongside I slid open the van door with a rope in my hands. Driving slowly beside it, I readied myself to wrap the rope around the dog's neck. But, before I could make a move it lunged at me first with teeth bared, slobbering, dry nostrils flaring. I jumped involuntarily onto Krishna Kaant's lap, shaking like a leaf while trying to slam the door shut. I kept pounding the monster's head and neck with the door as it snapped an inch from my leg, drooling, snarling, trying to get at me.

Somehow, finally, I got the door closed and just sat there in shock until Krishna Kaant asked me to remove myself from his lap. I said something lame about suspecting that was the dog we were looking for. It was time to change our plan, and next week I'll tell you what happened.

76. *Evil Dogs, Part Two*

It was almost with a sense of relief that I read that the Hindu priest, who had performed a marriage ceremony between a fourteen-year old girl to a pooch, was arrested. India's a strange land. There's no denying that. But, I read recently how a man in the U. S. was convicted of beating up a dog because he thought it was a homosexual. How strange is that? He was upset that the dog, a Poodle-Yorkshire terrier mix, repeatedly tried to engage in sexual activity with another male dog, a Jack Russell terrier.

Our story thus far: a mad dog mangled Amy and we had to find out if the animal was rabid. We discovered that several other people of the area had been bitten, a few ending up in the hospital, one or two in critical condition. Several teams went in search of the beast. After our first scary encounter with the animal, my buddy Krishna Kaant and I had to rethink our plan.

Meek, mild-mannered Krishna Kaant, who wouldn't hurt a fly, and I, with knees knocking together, dropped our ropes and picked up clubs. We had to do it for Amy. I was compelled to drive because the driver took a runner. First he looked as though he'd seen a ghost. Then he chortled on in strange tongues something about Ma Kali, the demon goddess. And then he bolted.

When next we caught sight of the monster-dog, I parked nearby and, as Krishna Kaant circled around, I stayed behind it near the van. Without a hint whatsoever that it even knew we were in the area, the dog whirled around and pounced … on the van. The crazy son of a bitch began gnarling the fender fiercely, furiously, ferociously, as though it were a living thing. He or she threw itself at the van again and again with complete and insane hatred. We thought it best not to interfere, to let them work it out for themselves; and, anyway, by then we knew we were way out of our depth.

A few minutes later, the dog began staggering down the road towards the main market area with the two of us following at a safe and respectful, if not cowardly, distance behind. It was late, and the streets were mostly empty. We realised that all we could reasonably do was warn people to get out of the way. But, up ahead in the distance we spotted a group of five policemen. I began yelling in Hindi that a mad dog was approaching. "Paagal kutta! Paagal kutta aayay! Paagal kutta!" The police fanned out across the street in anticipation of the dog's approach, twirling their batons. And then we saw a remarkable sight.

When the creature came close, it began to charge toward one of the policemen. But the cop flung his baton hard and with unbelievable accuracy. I never knew they had such skill with those sticks. It continued to twirl in the air and smacked the dog square in-between its wild eyes. The dog fell back and, with a second perfect strike by a second policeman, the dog collapsed. The five of them then proceeded to stone it to death showing no mercy whatsoever.

Would but that were the end of the story, but it ain't the end. We decided that I'd drive back to have a word with Dr Gaurav while Krishna Kaant guarded the carcass of the dog. There was really no question the animal had been rabid. There was surely no need for tests. But we thought we should at least ask. So after the police wandered off, well satisfied with their night's work and happy to let us clean up the mess. I drove back to Amy's place and was greeted like a hero.

Meanwhile, as one and all were warmly congratulating me, Krishna Kaant sat near the dog waiting. He closed his tired eyes and began to meditate, until he heard a strange gurgling noise. He looked up just in time to see his worst nightmare manifesting in front of him. He was completely, utterly alone, and the monster had climbed back to its feet, angry, staggering towards him. Krishna Kaant ran a few yards down the road in near total panic. Then he somehow collected himself. He picked up a boulder and walked back to where the dog was half up and half down on the roadside, plucked up his courage, and finished the job.

77. Toilet Survey, Part One

My friend Lucille wrote me an e-mail a few months back thanking me lavishly for sending along a few of my articles to her in Toronto. I felt great. I felt big. But then she added how my 'constant, incessant, moronic' mentioning of all things urinary made her feel sick. I could see her point, of course, so I responded in mature fashion by suggesting she pick herself up a good catheter and leave me alone. I stopped sending her my articles, even though I haven't used one story about peeing, or such bodily functions as would cause her illness, since.

Enough, however, is enough. I have to consider everyone's best interests; and I've been feeling for a long time now that there's a real need for an in-depth investigative report on the bathrooms of Wakefield. Lord knows someone has to raise the lid on this issue, and it may as well be me. Due to a lack of space, of course, it'll have to be a two-part series, at least.

The first place available for a good wiz, upon leaving the comforts of my own home, is the old fireplace half-way down the Rockhurst hill. It's a red brick affair standing free and unencumbered where a house must've surrounded it at some point in time. There's nothing quite like lifting one's leg there as one trundles down into the bowels, if you will, of Wakefield Village proper. The birds chirp, the squirrels squirrel and you don't need to get the key from smug-looking lady at the counter. To that old fireplace I award a full five stars, unless it's raining, of course, and then it slips to a one and a half.

Next, one comes to Hamilton's Chevrolet Dealership and its well-equipped facilities with lots of legroom, hot and cold running water, tiles, and towelling. The folks there are warm and welcoming, and the only reason I'm not awarding Hamilton's loo a full-fledged five is because it's better to remain a little anal retentive at car dealerships as a rule. Otherwise, you end up driving away a brand spanking new Jimmy, having left your old dump behind. I'll give it a four.

Everyone knows the latrines of India can get pretty rank, but they've got nothing over the Johnny-on-the-spots in the parks along the river, especially late in the season. They're hardly rateable nor really to be visited unless under extreme duress. Which is precisely why I miss them when they're taken away each winter; and so, just for adding to my general comfort level, I hand them three and a half stars.

As ratty as latrines can be in India, there are also some of the most elaborate in the world. Some have marble throughout, ornate fountains, and sofas, even attendants. My teacher was once asked to give a talk at the Taj Hotel in New Delhi, and I tagged along. I got a little cranky, however, when I found myself left way in the back behind hundreds of people listening, far away from the stage and Swami. Some of his main students were asked to speak, but not me. I eventually slipped out.

The latrine at the hotel was exotic. It was tiled from top to bottom in pristine white marble and it included a fountain and a statue. As I stood at the urinal, letting go of my negativity, in pranced Swami himself. I was startled to see him. The moment he stood next to me time, and everything else, stopped. I said, "Swami, now that you're here I can't pee." Not the most profound, philosophical way to break the silence, but he said, "Never mind. Give me a kiss instead. Which meant of course that one minute I was put off at him for leaving me out of the whole show and the next minute I was standing at the urinals with him and supposedly about to kiss while holding our respective willies.

I did lean toward him. And he certainly seemed poised to give me a big wet one. But my innate uptightness inhibited me from leaning far enough over. We both sort of kissed the air in the right general direction, he laughed uproariously as he bounded out of the crystal white room, and I was left to figure out what had just happened.

Next week, Chez Eric, the Alpengruss, even the train station latrines will be reviewed. But, for now I'll sign off with a reminder to drink lots of water and not to sprinkle on bushes in the city. People there tend to get easily pissed off. Needless to say, I'll be sending this article first to Lucille.

78. Toilet Survey, Part Two

It has been my intention to do a survey of Wakefield's latrines pretty much as my colleague, Will McLelland, did on poutines of the area. That recent investigative piece in The News sent shockwaves through the community. Poutine and latrines, I feel, have a symbiotic relationship, in fact and, like Will, I do harbour a hope that I may exert a positive influence on our community.

To that end, the next stop on our tour is a latrine in Wakefield's only strip mall, the one which houses Sandy's Famous Pizza, the gym, Salon Select Hairdressers and The Canada Pawn Shop, not to mention the public telephone that works for a nickel.

Although there's plenty of leg room in the washroom, tiles and paper towelling, it also has a few distinguishing features. The door to the place is always wide open, for example; and the door to the toilet, as well, had no latch 'til recently. But, what really sets it apart is the fact that a green garbage bag covered the urinal for at least two years, that being the full length of time I've lived in Wakefield. And now, a wooden box, painted white, seems to have been built to take its place.

The open door thing doesn't bother me at all. The latch to the actual toilet has been fixed, and the white, wooden box built to cover the urinal only adds a certain quirky charm to the place. You can always use the sink, if you get my drift. You may enter anytime without a dime. No need for a key. It gets four stars from me.

There was a time in India when I was being plagued by various exotic, pesky parasites. Eventually, one local doctor declared himself capable of testing for intestinal critters and, although the treatment was in some ways worse than the problem, we had little choice. People from the ashram would bring him a matchbox full of 'stuff' in the morning and phone for their results later the same day, even though the accuracy of his testing was always rather in doubt.

Dr Ahuja was old even back when I first went to India. And he had the hairiest ears any of us had ever seen. It was hard to keep one's eyes from wandering over to those big, hairy ears during a consultation. He first gained popularity among the ashram people by prescribing a certain Ayurvedic tonic for stomach disturbances that turned out to be highly alcoholic. Scores of boys and girls, who had taken vows against the use of any intoxicants, were guzzling booze unknowingly, staggering around the hills talking about Dr Ahuja's miracle cure and how much better they were feeling.

Somehow, he remained our physician of choice through the years, which goes a long way in describing the medical situation up there in those days. On one memorable occasion, I filled a matchbox with peanut butter instead of 'stuff' and delivered it in the morning. Later that day I phoned. As he answered the ring, our conversation went like this; "This is Dr Ahuja." "Gesundheit." "Aye?" "Bless you." "Bless you too. This is Dr Ahuja." "Gesundheit." "Aye?" "Never mind. This is Mr Nathan. Did you test my stuff?" "Yes, Mr Nathan. I found you have amoebas." "Oh." "Come tomorrow and receive some medicine please." "OK" "Good bye." "Good bye."

Then there was the time I scootered to town with my matchbox full of real 'stuff', labelled, ready to leave with the good doctor, only to discover that the clinic was closed. Not wanting to carry the stuff around all day, I decided to throw it in the river. Unfortunately, my aim was a little off. The trajectory wasn't what it should've been, and the matchbox, with my name and address clearly written on it, went straight in through someone's sitting room window. Well, obviously, I couldn't leave it lying on their sofa, so I climbed up the outside stairs, over a railing and crawled in through the window. I could see people in the next room as I stole back my matchbox and slunk out and down to the street shaking and sweating.

Meanwhile, of course, I'd been spotted. Some men grabbed me while I walked along; they took me to the police station, and I had to produce from my pocket what I'd stolen. And the rest, as they say, is history.

79. Temper Temper

When I was a boy, I looked to all the world quite mild-mannered, good-natured, even a little meek. Nothing, however, could've been further from the truth. If pushed just a little too far, I'd turn into a raving lunatic. It wouldn't matter how big or burly my adversary might be I'd lose all sense of control, not to speak of decorum.

Nine times out of ten my opponent would be a chair, door, or some such inanimate object, which was just as well because then at least I'd have a chance of winning. But, the basic fact was indisputable. I had a terrible temper. Fortunately, I got interested in the science of meditation and the pursuit of all things spiritual somewhere along the way. And many years of quiet, even silent contemplation of my navel left me changed, though not totally, along with a fairly lint-free belly button.

During my time in India, travelling with our guru and spiritual teacher on a day-trip up to the higher reaches of the Himalayan Mountains was considered a tremendous boon. We'd drive in a convoy to where the air was rare, the snow fell in heaps, and sages had meditated through the centuries impervious to the cold. Taking the same trip with just one friend and our teacher in his car, of course, was even more special.

One morning as I strolled along the road from my house, Swami's car stopped and his driver asked me to get in. Swami was sitting in the back seat, and we headed north for the day. We stopped beside mountain streams and water falls, walked through the passes and sat in wooden tea-stalls sipping hot, spiced tea. We laughed together, listened to Swami talk about the one life we all are, and asked him many questions. It was a magical, mystical time.

Having returned by evening, I sat down at a roadside café with some folks who were asking about my special day. And I was only too happy to tell them, except someone was revving up a motorcycle right next to us. I called over for the man to be quiet, but he didn't listen. He just kept on. I called out again, but my shouts fell on deaf ears. So I got up from my chair and walked over. I told the fellow to either leave or shut the damned thing off. He looked me straight in the eyes and revved the engine even more. I went nuts. I threw the bastard off his motorcycle and jumped on him before several people pulled me off. And so ended a beautiful day meditating in the mountains.

By the time I left India I assumed I'd transcended my less illustrious qualities and began my new life in Canada, in Wakefield. A long-time acquaintance, who lived in Chelsea, offered me some words of encouragement. "Nathan," she said. "You won't last the winter. Go away now." I was determined to prove her wrong, though it so happened I did discover that winters in Wakefield have a way of humbling you.

One howling, frigid day during that first winter, for example, it became abundantly clear that my holding tank needed to be emptied. Don't ask me how I knew. But, the ever-reliable Mr Dubois agreed to come and help, even in the blizzard. He only asked that I be sure to locate the top of the tank from under the snow in advance of his arrival. So I went out to where I knew the tank to be and began digging. It wasn't there. I shifted a few feet over and began again. It wasn't there either. My hands were freezing, my face burned from the cold, but I shuffled over a few feet more and began yet again. Still, no luck. I moved from place to place until eventually I just snapped. I took the shovel and started whacking the snow and ice like a total madman swearing in English and French, though I swore in French twice as loud as English in accordance with language laws. I was completely out of control, slashing the ground as if I were fourteen years old again. Then I looked up and saw my neighbour watching from beside his house. He was gawking open-mouthed in disbelief. And, after our eyes met, he quickly slipped back inside and bolted the door.

At times like those now I always remember the soothing, encouraging words of my teacher. On more than one occasion he said "Nathan, you're totally unsuited to this work. Go away now." Actually, what he really said was; "Nathan, keep meditating, keep praying, do good things and be patient. Remember how far we've come."

80. She's A Lady

I always feel strangely good after a prostate examination. I mean, it's just reassuring to know I'm all right.

Having decided it was once again time to probe the state of my over-all well being, I arranged an appointment with a doctor at the University of Ottawa Medical Centre. He came highly recommended and, unlike a certain clinic closer to home, was even willing to accept a new patient. When I arrived at the place, a long form on a clipboard was handed over for me to fill out. Several patients, mostly young students from the university, were waiting in the room.

Off to one side sitting alone, however, was a rather scanky-looking lady, long and thin with copious amounts of dark make-up around dark eyes covered somewhat by lengths of dark hair. She wore black high heeled shoes, short grey skirt, low-cut grey sweater showing plenty of cleavage, and a black vampire's cape. She had well-turned ankles, though her legs and arms were a tad muscular, and a masculine sort of jaw line.

Of course it occurred to me she might be a he, but she had breasts. I know breasts when I see them and she had some. Seeing that character, with her make-up, skirt and muscular arms, made me recall the sect of men in India who go from shop to shop dressed for all the world as women. They'd chant religious songs and dance around like minstrel maidens expecting each shop-keeper to cough up a few rupees, which they often did just to get rid of them. They symbolised the androgynous nature of each personification of God within the Hindu pantheon. The basic tenet of their belief was simply that God was male and female both, a form of non-duality, of oneness.

Since I'd neglected to bring glasses, I had to hold the questionnaire at arm's length. And even then, due to its ridiculously small print, I had a deuce of a time reading it. The lady across the room in that vampire's cape called to me in a gravelly voice. She offered to read the questions for me. So I shifted to a chair beside hers while people around the room peeked from above their magazines.

That lady learned as much about me in those few minutes as just about anyone in the region has in two years. She learned, for example, that I had my tonsils removed as a child and how my mommy brought ice cream afterward. I noticed a couple of young girls giggling together while looking over at us, but my new friend paid them no mind. She learned I'd had malaria twice, jaundice and hepatitis. She'd had hepatitis too.

Before I could check the 'no' box for whether I'd ever suffered depression, a nurse came and called my friend's name, inviting her in for some sort of hormone injection. So I was left alone, feeling actually just slightly depressed, and I never even got her phone number.

A couple of days later I went back to the clinic to drop off a sample which the doctor had asked me to collect in a small plastic container. I'd put the container containing the sample in a fancy 'Godiva's Chocolates' bag, which I thought was a nice touch. There in the waiting room, sitting all alone as before, was my friend wearing the same black cape and low-cut sweater. She smiled at me, but I noticed her arms and legs were all scraped up. She said she'd been pushed around by a group of local boys. I asked why. She merely shrugged her shoulders, saying it was probably just because she's different.

I left again without her number. Of course I didn't actually want it. But, I recalled a Jesse Winchester song that goes: ' Now when I look at myself, I'm a stranger by my birth.' And as I drove away from the clinic that morning, nearly running over a small Asian boy, it occurred to me that the one sitting alone in her cape, with scrapes all over her body, really had been a lady.

81. Weekend Blessings

On Saturday the 30th of September I walked to work as I usually do, dressed as I usually am in sport shirt, Levi's, baseball cap and a pair of fairly new Nikes, like any common street-person. Toddling along, minding my own business, I stumbled upon an empty black purse on the sidewalk in front of Holt Renfrew's.

Of course I understand that purses do end up empty after a visit to Holt-Renfrew's, but they're not usually discarded outright. There was some make-up, lipstick, a small jar of cream, a package of condoms and a set of keys lying nearby. Nothing of any use to me, of course, but it was irksome to think a lady was out there somewhere upset. Some bad person had rummaged around in that purse, taken the wallet and run off to Macdonald's for an Egg-McMuffin. And, as I bent over to take a closer look, a policeman drove up, told me to get against the wall and spread my legs wide. Well, actually, as I bent over the purse, a fellow walking by mistook me for the robber and called me an animal. There was no address to be found in or around the purse, so I just left everything and carried on to my place of worship, if work is indeed worship, which I often doubt.

I was invited to a wedding in town that same night. Not having had time even for a break all day, I rushed to the ceremony and then, bagged, drove up to the Jumpa Restaurant past Edelweiss for the dinner and reception. It was noisy, I didn't really know anyone, and I was seated facing a wall. Each table of people in the restaurant was required to get up and sing a love song, after which the bride and groom would kiss. One table's performance was so good, however, I thought it deserved more than just a simple kiss, perhaps a little tongue action or some fondling, but I keep my thoughts to myself.

The folks at my table decided to do a song that, of course, I'd never heard of, along with a little dance of sorts such as The Temptations or The

Supremes used to do. At a certain juncture we were supposed to point at our eyes, then cover our hearts, then point to the bride and groom as we sang, 'I love you.' I didn't do too badly, really, although I did get a bit confused, pointed at my ears instead of my eyes and saw some people laughing. Nevertheless, I figure they were damn lucky I didn't point to my crotch instead of my heart during the love part. I felt I'd done well.

Next day, Sunday, on October 1st, I took my cat, Morris, to the Blessing of Animals on the Feast of St. Francis of Assisi at Holy Trinity Church in Lascelles. The only thing I'd ever heard about St. Francis of Assisi was that he lived in the 13th century and became so frustrated trying to stay celibate that he snipped off his willy. Certainly, as an ex-Buddhist monk I sympathised with him. I've entertained some pretty wild thoughts while slicing tofu sausages for breakfast back in those days. It's no surprise to me that St. Francis became fond of all things soft and furry. Having said all that, I should add that I've recently been told, rather emphatically, that he didn't really cut it off.

It was encouraging to see how relaxed Morris remained as we drove up from Wakefield to Pritchard's Road. His whiskers began twitching and his eyes widened as we approached the church and he heard a cacophony of snarling and barking getting louder and louder the closer we got. By the time we arrived, of course, his face had become a mask of sheer terror. Still, whatever trauma Morris suffered, it was a small price to pay for getting blessed.

In the yard, all manner of beasts had gathered. There were cats, goats, a horse, some guinea pigs, one or two gerbils and countless fleas all ready for their blessing. Mostly, there were dogs of all shapes and sizes howling, lunging at each other's throats, and sniffing each other. The last time I saw anything like it was at a wine and cheese party up on Parliament Hill after question period. I was a struggling young reporter then, but that's another story.

Clearly, I'm not even being fair. Reverend Peter John Hobbs honestly created a charming occasion again this year of both fun and enlightenment. His words concerning the importance of taking care of God's creatures, God's creation, have stayed with me like a warm blanket on cold autumn nights. And I'm quite sure Morris will eventually come out of the broom-closet.

82. For All Time To Come

Following six months of driving repeatedly to a village north of my home, the council was finally ready to hear my offer. The stone carving I wanted was mostly buried in the side of the Himalayan Mountains. It had been neglected for decades, obscured by the ground and brush, and largely forgotten. But, so far they'd refused to let me have it.

Standing approximately seven feet high, the stone slab was rounded at the top. There was a low-relief carving of Lord Shiv on its surface. He had strange, bug eyes and a snake wrapped around his neck. It was a Sutti stone, made to honour a lady who'd thrown herself, or who'd been thrown, onto her husband's funeral pyre. I liked the carving, its intricate detail and the thought that I was saving it from being lost forever.

The village elders had been reluctant to release the tablet, especially to a white-faced foreigner, and I took months to convince them it wouldn't be leaving the district, let alone the country. Fortunately, I was pretty well known in the district, and the village was fully involved in the massive reconstruction of their local temple. They needed money. I offered a size-able 'donation' in return for the stone and, a week later, I drove back up with tractor, chains, ropes. Several villagers began digging the thing out of the mountainside. I was happy. I felt like Indiana Jones. After much toil the stone was finally freed. However, as they leaned it forward a huge snake slithered out from behind.

The villagers threw their collective arms up in the air, dropped the stone, their tools and all semblance of composure and ran screaming and yelling, to cower under their beds at home. A snake hanging anywhere around a statue of Lord Shiv was considered all kinds of bad luck. I knew I had to get the stone into the tractor and away before the elders decided they'd made a horrible, unlucky mistake. At any moment they'd realize they may have angered Shiv, the God of destruction.

My driver, the tractor man and I managed somehow to chain the thing and pull it up onto the tractor. We set it on a bed of straw and took the two hour trip back to my place. I decided not to put the statue in my gallery, but cart it all the way up the hillside to my house. It wasn't easy. A mason was then called on to fit it into the stone wall of my bedroom. That was the culmination of many months' work. I lit candles in front of the carving, letting the shadows dance around the room. Only then, as I lay back on my bed and gazed at the figures, could I really take it in.

For the first time, since the ground had largely hidden it, I could see the whole thing. And I realised it was actually quite freaky. Lord Shiv's face looked like E. T.'s, with bug eyes and a very weird grin. He had a snake around his neck and was sitting cross-legged on a bull. From between his legs there appeared a temple, long, thin, like a male organ; and he was pouring clarified butter from a jug onto it.

The over-all effect was obviously phallic and unsettling, even repulsive. I tried to change my feelings. I tried to change my mind. I knew the carving was meant as a religious depiction of love and devotion in some primal way. After two days and nights, however, I insisted it be taken away. I asked the same men who put it in to take it out. Call me picky, but I just didn't want to watch Shiv maniacally doing what it was he was obviously doing in the corner of my bedroom for all time to come, excuse the expression.

The next day I had the stone dragged back down to the road side, put back on the same tractor, driven back to the village, and returned to its original place. And there I left Lord Shiv to do his own thing in the privacy of his own home.

83. Decriminalise Marijuana, or Going to Pot

It felt really good to participate in the recent heartfelt support extended to the charming Andrea Criten. She's very special. Local businesses organised the dance to help offset a staggering financial burden her family's been labouring under since Andrea fell ill with cancer. The feelings were deep, the music was jumping but it was slightly unsettling, under the circumstances, to spend half the night hacking from secondary smoke inhalation.

I'm not against smoking. My own mom's been smoking since she was about four. She just had her eighty-second birthday, and she can still put the fear of God into me. Mom and dad still play golf regularly. Dad hits the ball and mom tells him where it's gone. And she carries both bags. Sure, I'm kidding about her carrying the bags, but not about her strength in spite of smoking all those years.

I'm aware that there are all different types of addiction. I have a buddy who was addicted to gambling. He used to head to Las Vegas every chance he'd get, take Ecstasy and play Blackjack. One time, he was peaking on Ecstasy just as he won a large pot of money and fell off his chair backwards.

A friend at my place of work in Ottawa recently handed me some green leaves for Morris, the cat who lets me live with him. I'd heard of catnip, but had never actually seen any. When Morris greeted me that night as usual with a nice snuggle, he nudged my pocket, reminding me I had a treat for him. So I dumped the whole bag of catnip on the floor in front of him.

He fell on the stuff like a cat possessed. Seeing his reaction, I grabbed some for myself, snorted a bit, rubbed it around my gums, but it did nothing for me. On the other hand, it was a little scary to watch Morris.

His eyes glazed over, he rolled on the leaves and began bouncing from wall to wall. He ran up and down the stairs, made lewd gestures at the electric can opener before falling in a lifeless heap on the carpet. I monitored his pulse through the night.

Some friends have tried to convince me that even I have a problem, and I've not been out and about much for almost ever. They say I'm strung out on butter, which is quite ridiculous, of course. I could quit any time I want and, by definition, that means I'm not addicted. It's just that there was no good butter for most of my twenty-three years in India. There was only a rather acrid sort of clarified butter known as ghee. Since my return, some two years ago now, I suppose I've indulged myself; but I hardly think my enjoying a little butter warrants the constant badgering I receive at the hands of relatives and friends.

My dad and I were sitting across from each other one morning recently during breakfast when I simply asked him to pass the butter. It was not a complicated request. He peered critically over at me from above his spectacles and said I eat far too much of the stuff for my own good. He lectured me at length on the dangers of cholesterol. I thought for a moment or two, then said "Dad, I don't eat red meat, chicken or fish. I don't smoke or take recreational drugs of any sort. I steer clear of headache pills. I've rarely ever had any alcohol in my life and sex even less. Pass the fucking butter."

Now, I have no doubt that those who read page four of The News on a regular basis will be expecting me to end by saying I'm addicted to love, or something lame like that. And I would. But I won't, because I haven't had my first cup of coffee yet this morning. However, as I squinted through a smoky haze recently at a vibrant, brave, lovely young Andrea Criten joking with friends gathered round her, I knew myself to be, in fact, incredibly high on life.

84. We Have All Been Here Before

Do you believe in reincarnation? I know for a fact I've been here before. In 1979 I had to leave India for a while due to a severe paucity of funds. I had no money. Broke. Zilch. Nada. And so I just assumed I'd head back to the gulf islands off British Columbia's coast where I had lived for several years prior to my heading off to the Far-East, and where I had managed to live by writing, tree-planting and house-sitting. But, I was offered a room with a view in an Ottawa meditation centre, and I was inclined to accept. I just wanted to ask my teacher's opinion first.

It was then the festival of Guru Poornima, during which all spiritual teachers are honoured across India. And as I waited in a long line-up that day to garland Swamiji, I couldn't help noticing how most people managed a few words of conversation with him during their turns. Some were having full-fledged conversations, chatting, laughing and posing for the video camera. I also couldn't help noticing how each person initiated his/her interaction with Swami.

Of course I wanted to bring up the subject of my going to Ottawa, but it didn't seem appropriate. So I wondered what to say. I didn't want to be the only jerk to garland him, then kneel in the age-old customary fashion before just speechlessly fading away. I decided I'd simply say that he was looking good and see what that might lead to. As I inched toward the front of the line, I practised my sentence over and over in my mind. "You're looking especially good today, Swamiji. You're looking Especially lovely, Swamiji. You're Really looking very good today, Swamiji." Obviously, it was ridiculously overdone, but I did want the moment to go off without a hitch. People were watching. Cameras were trained on the scene.

I goose-stepped closer to the front, repeating my sentence almost involuntarily again and again silently, until there remained no one between us. I moved up with my garland, shiny purple, green and silver tinsel with its little red tassel, and draped it over his head. I knelt down and was about to blurt out my line when Swamiji said "How are your parents these days?" Taken totally by surprise, I said they were fine, a little too loudly I thought. I was beginning to stand when he continued. "Have you heard from them lately?" I felt as though I shouted that I'd spoken to them by phone just the day before. By then I was on my feet, flushed, ready to move on. Swamiji, however, had other ideas. He asked how my cousins were doing since their recent visit to India. I turned back, even more flustered while the cameras rolled, and positively barked that my cousins were fine and that they write often, which was totally wrong. And then, as I scuttled further away, I heard Swamiji call after me "By the way, you're looking especially lovely today."

Later that same evening I sneaked into Swamiji's tiny, wooden pyramid that he'd built for his private meditation. I used to sneak into it from time to time, which was rather cheeky of me. And, as I thought about what it'd be like in Ottawa, Swamiji came crawling in through the little door. But, he didn't mind that I was there. He just smiled and said we could meditate together. Meanwhile, I was consumed by a desire to ask his opinion of my plans. All through the meditation I could think of nothing else. Eventually, as we sat in the dark and silent pyramid, I heard him let out a deep breath and say; "Ask me your question, Nathan, for heaven's sake." So I told him the situation, and he readily agreed it'd be a great move. Then he said, "Can we meditate now?"

As I hugged Swamiji good-by a few short days later, holding back a tear, he whispered that I should always remember that the teacher lives inside my own head and heart. And that every time I care to look, I'll find him looking back.

85. Leap Before You Look

It's still a mystery why I decided to leave India. In fact, I didn't leave India. I merely decided not to return. There's a difference. There were no possessions, no plan, and no turning back. Something called to me as I floated across the Atlantic, and I knew I just had to take a chance at a new life.

It's been my pattern to jump into the unknown without much fore-thought. That's the real mystery. Faced with a choice to play it safe or go for the big score, take a dangerous risk to find the perfect artefact, friend, house, life, I've always known I really should play it safe. And then I've gone off half cocked anyway, often with disastrous results. During my first high-school basketball game, for example, I was the first person to handle the ball after the first toss. I dribbled over centre court properly, but when it came time to make that first pass, instead of doing the right thing, the safe pass, I chose a completely unnecessary, fancy, behind-the-back manoeuvre. Predictably, it went horribly wrong, way up into the stands and landed, coincidentally, in my best friend's lap. The coach sat my sorry back-side down on the bench for the rest of the game, and I never entirely recovered the rest of the season. In fact, that turned out to be the high-point of my career.

Last Monday I was reminded yet again of how I haven't really changed much since that basketball game. I saw one of the loveliest chairs I'd ever seen lying right at the end of a village driveway. I couldn't believe someone could just discard such a thing of beauty. So, of course I decided to grab it for myself. I could've just gone to the door and asked if it'd be alright to take the chair away. I even knew the people. I'm sure I could've just gone ahead and taken the thing. Instead, without really thinking, I skulked back under cover of darkness to steal it like a coward.

I drove up beside the driveway, turned the lights off and opened the trunk of my car. I wore black clothes, gloves and a baseball cap turned backwards. Unfortunately, just as my hot hands grabbed the chair, a six-thousand watt over-head lamp went on and the lady of the house came out. She was just heading for the wood pile, but I panicked. I jumped in the car and drove with headlights off and trunk wide-open, empty and flapping all the way home.

As far as I was concerned, that was the end of the misadventure. And yet, as the clock struck one in the morning, I couldn't resist returning to try again. In the very dark of night, when all things living should really be in trees, under rocks, in bed or in jail, I spirited the chair away. I scraped my arm. I tweaked my back. But I got that chair quickly into my living room and turned on the light to finally take a good look. It certainly had been a fine and proud beauty in its day. Its day, however, had long passed, and I could see it clearly for what it was: a smelly, musty, dirty, torn old chair that badly wanted throwing away. I'd done it again.

I've heard that some personality quirks never go away, even if a person becomes a Buddha, a Christ, a Krishna. Still, having said all that, I should add I've had more than my share of good luck when it counted most. Running off to India, for example, was a tremendous chance to take. And instead of finding myself I found the self, the one self or the one life permeating all. You may have already known that, but I got lucky. Now I know too.

Two years after leaping once again into the unknown, to live in Canada, in Wakefield, I walk through the village in all its autumnal splendour and am quite sure I've been so very fortunate. Bumping into the likes of Mike, Ian, Paul, Mary, Mark or Lori while tiptoeing beside the river's edge, shooting hoops at the school surrounded by showering orange leaves, I know I've won big-time this time, again.

86. Where Have All The Flowers Gone?

If you perused by chance the pages of the Ottawa Sun on August 10, you may have noticed an article with the catchy little headline 'Duped For Diamonds'.

The article starts out with the equally catchy line, 'If diamonds are a girl's best friend, one Middle Eastern woman has no fear of ever being lonely.' It goes on to describe how a man and woman have stolen hundreds of thousands of dollars worth of diamonds from stores in Montreal, Toronto and Ottawa. Later in the article, it's written that 'another jeweller, hearing about the incidents, called police claiming the scoundrels had attempted their trickery in his store, and the surveillance camera caught them on video tape.' That store was the one in which I walk round and round eight hours every day.

A particular frame from the video was carefully chosen for widespread publication in various newspapers in all three cities. It was chosen because it clearly shows the faces of the culprits. Unfortunately for me, it also clearly shows the large bald spot on the back of the head of the 'diamond sales consultant.' So, now thousands of folks have had a real good look at my bald spot. Isn't that marvellous? Just the other day a lady stopped me on the street and said she recognised me from the newspaper and asked if I'd turn around just to make sure. That didn't actually happen, but I'm certain you understand how I feel. I've been not duped out of diamonds so much as duped out of my rightful fifteen minutes of fame.

I remember the first time I noticed my hair getting thin. There was a local barber in India who would cut your hair for the equivalent of fifty cents, trim your beard for less than about twenty-five cents and/or perform a head and shoulders massage for whatever you wanted to give. I never cut my hair or beard in those days, but I went in once for the head and shoulders massage special.

The barbershop was a barbaric one by western standards, with newspaper cut outs of Hindi movie stars plastered all over the wood-plank walls, benches made of wood planks, and wood planks serving as counters. One bit of the décor the barber didn't scrimp on, however, was mirrors. There were mirrors all over the place. And one was strategically placed on the wall behind, slanted perfectly to offer a panoramic view of the back of one's head. When I noticed my encroaching baldness, I was horrified. It put me right off the massage, and I'm afraid I was none too generous with the fellow, as if somehow it were his fault.

It's not as if I haven't enjoyed copious amounts of the stuff in my life. I was at Woodstock. Well, I wasn't really, but I've had lots of hair. It's just that the way I'm balding is so odd. It's the laurel wreath effect, like Curley from the Three Stooges. There's no way I'd ever consider getting a transplant or wearing one of those awful rugs. I'd rather look strange than stupid. And I suppose I shouldn't dwell on hair so much or I may re-incarnate as a Yak.

Still, while merchants from all over the region are worrying about where the diamonds have gone from their stores, I'm helplessly worrying about truly important matters. I wasn't even really suspicious of that couple that came to steal diamonds. In fact, I would've offered a few to the lady just to watch her walk around the place. She had quite a walk. No, I'm wondering who stole the hair from that spot at the back of my head. Pete Seeger's worrying about who's taken his banjo from his car. These things are important. Of course, in the end one has little choice but to accept one's lot, laugh at life, and put what little remains of one's hair in a ponytail.

87. Cheapest And Best

For my first several years in India, like so many westerners I was amazed and not a little gratified to discover how inexpensive the living was. A full dinner could be twenty-five cents, a month's rent was five dollars, a shirt and pantsuit would run you a buck.

Slowly, however, the realisation seeped into my consciousness that one does tend to get what one pays for. Duh. It started seeping during the first week I was in India, during dinner at a local eatery. I was pleased as punch to gorge myself on vegetable curry, dahl and chapattis for less than a Slurpy back home. But, as I looked down innocently into my dahl, I spotted a cooked cockroach staring back up at me. And the look upon its face was as if he were saying "Oye! I zigged when I shoulda zagged!" It frankly put me right off my food.

It really began seeping when I rented a wonderfully cheap apartment that turned out to be so damp that my clothes never dried. Mould was growing on the walls and, while I counted my pennies saved, I got bronchitis regularly. The plumbing was tenuous, the electricity was off more than it was on. And then, of course, there was Beant Singh.

You could go to Beant Singh's shop to choose cloth, which would cost less than a pair of jockey shorts over here, and he'd tailor it into a shirt and pant-suit within a couple of hours. Unfortunately, the end result was usually un-fulfilling, not to mention un-fulfitting. I remember picking up a shirt there only to discover that one sleeve was longer than the other. When I mentioned the fact to Beant, he said I was standing wrong. He even demonstrated how I might correct my posture. There was another tailor in the village, but he only had one eye.

While strolling in the hills one day, I was offered sex for the bargain-basement price of a dollar by a toothless old mountain lady. And although some might argue that her being toothless was a plus, I found the whole situation rather unsettling. And speaking of toothless, the dentistry over there can be marvellously inexpensive, but I've already written about the dentistry.

Back in Canada after all those years, I've found a package of green garbage bags a good deal. They seem to last forever. Or perhaps I should be making more of a point to remember that Tuesday is garbage pick-up day. A certain telephone in the village, which works for a nickel, was a spectacular deal until an irresponsible reporter mentioned its location; and now I'm not sure it's even still available.

The best deal I've had since settling in the West, however, has been my watch. It's a Timex that I picked up in New York City, literally. I found it under a table in a funky Manhattan restaurant. The lady I was with felt very strongly that I turn the thing over to the management in case its owner returned to claim it. I acquiesced against my better judgement so as not to look like a cad. I liked the lady. I mean, I liked liked the lady ... and she wasn't even toothless.

Anyway, as it happened there were to be no stronger feelings from her that night than what she'd exhibited for the rightful owner of the watch. Nevertheless, being a sage-like yogi who'd spent his formative and middle years studying Vedic scriptures and practising meditation, I dealt with rejection wisely. I sneaked back to the restaurant alone before closing time, and inquired of a waitress if a Timex watch had been found. I described it, she smiled broadly, so glad she could help, and now every time I look at that watch I don't mind nearly so much the memory of that trip to New York City.

Everyone knows the best things in life are free: a smile from a neighbour, the river, the trees. You can freely stand tall and bark at the full moon no matter who's watching. You can love your lady, love your man, your brother, sister, cat, dog or gerbil without a nickel gone. But, the best deal still has to be good health. So be well, one and all.

88. *Swinging Doors*

The entrance doors to the shop where I work aren't exactly normal. It's actually a double entrance. For the sake of security, people have to walk in the first, wait 'til that one closes before going through the next into the store itself. The fun begins at door number two.

Folks don't exactly realize how to access the place, and so they rush through the first door at their normal clip, at break-neck speed, and push the second door, which of course doesn't budge. The first door hasn't closed. Then they become confused, disoriented and often begin to freak out. They try pulling door number two hard, harder, but that doesn't work. Then they push anything that looks like a button. They open the door to the furnace room, rush in, rush back out in growing panic, beads of sweat on their foreheads, in some cases close to tears.

By that time, of course, the first door has long since closed. So I, or some other employee inside, points reassuringly to the second door through the Plexiglas window. The people look doubtful. They often need to be coaxed, but eventually they take a chance to try the door one more time. And, needless to say, it opens. The people walk in wiping their eyes, broken, in a perfect state of mind, in fact, to purchase ridiculously expensive luxury merchandise.

My personal favourite scenario is when someone rushes in through the first door, goes crazy in all ways previously described, turns round to escape back out from whence they've come just as someone from inside the shop opens the door to leave. That means the person stuck between the two doors can't even open the first. As well, they find they're no longer alone, have no idea how that happened and, on very special occasions, accuses the other person of being an alien or at least subversive. In the end, of course, the situations always work themselves out, everyone recovers from the trauma, though often not without therapy and/or a new Rolex.

It would be an understatement to say village India never had such high-tech entrances. Of course, the major cities now have nearly all western accoutrements and sophisticated ways of stressing and aggravating the people. But, up in the mountains, where I grazed for most of my formative years, they're still backward. Quite often, in fact, doors don't even work. Once, an elevator was actually installed by an ambitious local hotelier and I was invited to attend the maiden voyage. We got stuck between floors, like, right away. It was the Titanic of elevators.

What you find in the villages even today are doorways made for rather shorter Homo sapiens than the average westerner. Lord Mountbatten was once quoted as saying, just after entering a temple on a state visit to the Himalayas and as he rubbed his head "Jesus Mary Murphy! What the dickens was that!?" And Queen Elizabeth, on a similar visit, in a similar situation, and similarly rubbing her head, was heard whispering to her aide de compte, "Why the hell don't they build these freaking doorways for people who stand up on their hind legs aye what?" or something to that effect. I've bumped into more crossbeams myself than Indian dogs have fleas. Maybe that's why I have that easy peaceful feeling. Maybe it's not meditation at all. Maybe I've wasted my whole adult life on meditation. Smacking ones head repeatedly on crossbeams is bound to have some effect after all.

Meanwhile, back on Sparks Street and speaking of easy peaceful feelings, I always know when Wakefielders or Wakefieldians are entering the shop. They're the only folks so laid back that, by the time they get to the second door, the first has actually closed. They probably never even know that the first door has to close before the second opens. It's just one more small reason why you gotta love this town.

89. *This Too Will Change*

Driving to Toronto after work on any given Saturday evening is a sure-fire way to induce an altered state of consciousness. By the time I arrive, I've figured out the meaning of life, have probably seen God more than once, and really dislike small red Audis.

After arriving in downtown Toronto last Sunday by two-thirty in the morning, I bedded down at a friend's place. As I unlocked my car in the morning, an odd looking fellow stepped up and asked if I knew how he could get to Toronto. I told him to hang a left at the next corner, and he staggered off in the general direction.

My folks had no idea I was coming. I phoned from across their street, but carried on a conversation with my dad just as we always do. We talked of golf, he asked when they could expect grandchildren and told me I should be demanding more money from my employers. I asked how the weather was there, and he said it was a miserable, cloudy day. He asked about the weather where I was and I said it was pretty much the same. I mentioned I wasn't in Wakefield and he asked where I was. I said I was in town, which of course meant Ottawa to him, visiting some special friends. After we said our good-byes, I walked across the street and knocked on their door. My dad took one look at me and collapsed, thrashed around on the ground for a few moments before lying still. From the back room, I could hear my mom call out, "David, who is it?"

Actually, what really happened was that, after our conversation, I crossed to their building and phoned up from the lobby. My mom answered. I said it was Nathan, to which she responded, "How can it be you? You just phoned from Ottawa." I said it was a joke and I've come to Toronto to see them. She wasn't at all sure she should let me in, but in the end I convinced her, gave her flowers as I entered, and it was hugs all round.

In India, there's a story of two brothers trundling along very different paths. When their father died, the more materialistic brother was left the whole estate. The other was given only a small cabin in a corner of the vast property, along with his father's ring. Many years went by in which the wealthy brother became increasingly unhappy and disillusioned. So one day he visited his brother and asked how he'd remained happy in spite of his poverty. The simple brother let out that his secret was the mantra he'd found inscribed inside their father's finger ring. It read: 'This Too Will Change.' He said that all through the years, through good or bad times, he always remembered that mantra; and so he'd learned to cultivate equanimity and contentment.

Last Sunday morning in Toronto we went out for brunch, to a place we always go, and I let the folks off in front of the restaurant. Before I could slip into a nearby parking space, a sleek, red, Audi cut in front. But, mom threw herself between the cars and hollered at the driver to bloody well find himself another space. The fellow probably realised it wasn't important why the old lady was gesticulating wildly in the middle of the parking lot. She was scary. He drove off and I slipped into the spot. The parking space being a tight fit, I first had to edge my way in on an angle. However, before I could even begin to straighten the car out my dad scuttled up and knocked on the window. "Straighten out the car!," he barked. "Don't leave it like this!"

Later, as I prepared to return to Wakefield, dad lectured me on my need to buy myself a razor and a book on English grammar, as usual. Mom packed me some muffins she'd had in the freezer since around 1937, as usual. After I had kissed them both goodbye, dad called out, "Surprise us again soon." And mom yelled down the hall "Just be happy!" as usual.

90. *Love Song Heaven*

There's a rather famous painting in India created by a rather famous painter named Shobha Singh. It depicts a lovely girl wearing a simple sari and shawl and holding a water jug. A handsome boy has an arm around her waist while the two run against the wind. Their expressions are as if they're either in love or in distress, which of course are quite similar.

The story behind the painting is of the girl, who was from a wealthy Sikh family, and the boy, who was a poor Hindu. They lived on opposite sides of a large lake and, although they were deeply in love, their families were against the match. In fact, eventually they were forbidden to meet. They'd gaze over at each other from opposite shores and, in the end, couldn't stand to stay apart. The boy began swimming toward the girl, but it was too far and he floundered. Seeing the boy in trouble, the girl swam out to him and they both drowned together in the middle of the lake.

There's a rumour that the boy, in a desperate attempt to save himself, actually pushed his girlfriend under, although I don't believe that. And some other cynics have expressed a certain incredulity that the couple didn't just commission a boat or a raft of some sort, but they're all missing the point. The two were in love. And that love transcended all differences. In fact, they wanted to be together so much that they were willing to die rather than stay apart.

The Lebanese poet Kahlil Gibran, of the early nineteen hundreds, wrote: 'Love one another, but make not a bond of love; let it rather be a moving sea between the shores of your souls.' I rather prefer what the fifteenth-century poet, Kabir, wrote about love. Born Hindu, raised as a Muslim, Kabir became a weaver and spun not only cloth but yarns that have endured through the ages. In one of his most famous love poems he wrote ' you can't live with them and you can't live with them.' That may not have been one of his most famous. He also wrote ' Why should we two ever want to part? This love between us goes back to the first humans. It cannot be annihilated. Here is Kabir's idea: As the river gives itself to the ocean, I give myself to you.'

True love transcends race, creed, and colour, even species. My cat Morris, for example, doesn't seem to care that I'm human. I'm not crazy about the way he gazes over at my lower haunches sometimes, but I feel tremendous love and affection for him, even though he's gained quite a bit of weight since we first got together. He was the best little mouser in the village back when he had that lean and hungry look. I saw him chase a mouse last night for the first time in ages. He lunged, tried to jump onto the counter and fell down rather heavily to the floor. It was pathetic. The mouse turned, looked down and laughed. Still, I adore my friend Morris.

'Inside her water jug there are canyons and pine mountains,' Kabir wrote. 'And the maker of canyons and mountains. All seven oceans are inside and hundreds of millions of stars. The acid that tests gold, the one who judges jewels and the music from the strings no one touches and the source of all water. If you want the truth, I will tell you, friend. Listen. God and the one I love are inside.'

91. Who Let The Dogs Out?

This is not a column. This is a state of mind and it's weird. Having been on heavy-duty antibiotics now for the past week, I'm not exactly thinking straight. Or, perhaps my thinking's always been so crooked that now it's straight. I'd like to rail against the medical profession, again, since it'd be trendy and these pills are killing me, only I'm actually hoping to rid myself of some fairly exotic parasites, and I don't mean the cat. I didn't bring the cat from India.

India's a land of magic, esoteric knowledge and self-realisation. It's also the land of poverty, child labour and parasites. And, as well, it's also the land of antibiotics where they're prescribed for everything from parasites to leprosy, from toothache to baldness. They're given as gifts for birthdays, breaded and deep-fried, even used as currency.

There was a time in India when I lost the hearing in my left ear, which I thought for a while was a result of opening latent mystic energies. I've written about this before. The point is that I was put on two different courses of anti-biotics and would've gone on about three more courses had I listened to every doctor I went to. And in the end, one crusty old doctor found a wax-covered piece of rolled-up tissue deep inside my ear. I'd put it in as an earplug at the New Delhi airport and forgotten about it.

The most severe and scary illness I have ever had was not mononucleosis or malaria, hepatitis or jaundice. It was an average, garden-variety bronchitis. I had such a nasty bout of it, I couldn't lie down for fear of choking to death. I'd wake up coughing, choking, and unable to catch a breath; three courses of different anti-biotics did nothing to alleviate the condition. When I was at my worst, I actually left my body. I was floating up around the ceiling and looking down at myself in the bed. Then I noticed another astral body floating next to me looking down at my body too. So I said, "Hey, what're you doin?" And he said, "I'm allowed to look."

Now, of course that never happened. But, I'll tell you what did happen. When I was at my worst, I woke up very late one night choking and trying to just catch one little breath. I couldn't. I was actually choking to death. I stumbled outside into the front yard spluttering and staggering, turning purple. My neighbours all came running from their beds, which choked me up even more. The Sikh lady I rented my cabin from kept repeating how she didn't know what to do. The Montreal lawyer, who was staying in her extra room, tried clapping me on the back until I waved him off. Both family dogs nudged my pockets hoping for cookies, which I thought rather insensitive. I was painfully aware that if I hadn't somehow squeaked in that first breath, there would've been no tomorrow, no Chez Eric, Earl House or Sandy's Pizza, no Wakefield in fact, no life as we know it for me.

That night I realised, as if for the first time, that you die alone. It's a harsh reality. No matter how many relations you have, no matter how many children or grandchildren, nobody goes with you at that time. That's one journey you make alone. So it behoves us each to ask the age-old questions; Where do I go at that time? Where did I come from? I know where this article's coming from. It's coming from Rockhurst Drive, which runs between River Road and Highway 105. That information may seem trivial to you, but it helps keep me from getting lost.

As I slip further into this antibiotic funk, I'll end today by wishing happiness on everyone. The dictionary says happiness 'is the enjoyment of pleasure.' So I looked up the word 'pleasure' and it read 'see happiness.' Therefore, I'll simply wish everyone, yet again and not for the last time, good health.

92. Progress

Not far from where I live, in the wild backwoods of the Rockhurst Rain Forests, stands a strange, almost sinister-looking, shack with electronic equipment attached and large spools of wire next to it. Curious, I asked a neighbour what it was, and he told me that as an outsider I'd do well to just mind my own business. Actually, he told me it was the local cable television operation. I was instantly transported back to a time in India when watching television slowly took the place of any sort of spiritual practice. Those were the days ...

A few of the local boys introduced me to Aney and asked if I'd help him start a business. I was only too happy to oblige. It's not that I was a great philanthropist. On the contrary, it was more to do with the fact that I hadn't watched any western television for over twenty years. And Aney wanted to start a satellite television business in the area.

The boys told me Aney had a very young family of three kids and an asthmatic wife. Since I was familiar with the dark, dank, damp dungeon room Aney had just moved his family into across the street, I instantly felt sorry for his poor wife. Of course, that was overshadowed by the positively giddy feeling I experienced at the possibility of watching NBA Basketball, Ally McBeale and CNN News on a regular basis.

In truth, as exciting as I found the idea, I couldn't help being sceptical. We knew the technology had come to India. I just personally had a problem believing it'd work up there in the mountains where one couldn't safely turn on a blender without the whole district blacking out. Even so, I told Aney that if it actually worked, I'd pay several months rent in advance as well as try to convince my friends to hook up.

For over two decades I, along with my white-faced expatriate friends, hadn't seen any English television. We'd only begun to receive India's one channel, in Hindi of course, a couple of years earlier. Needless to say, I watched that stuff anyway, rather religiously actually, even though I couldn't understand much. And the ridiculously poor reception made the figures seem as though they were belly dancing in a perpetual, howling blizzard.

After Aney and the boys left, I sat down to watch television as usual. Aney came in once to hook up a line and I just shook my head, feeling a little sad for the well-meaning, naïve young entrepreneur. I especially felt sorry for his asthmatic wife. About twenty minutes later, however, my television started acting funny until, all of a sudden, a show came on as crystal clear as the nose on my face. It was called, 'Santa Barbara.' I forgot all about Aney's wife. On television a beautiful, well-dressed couple sat sipping champagne together in a wood-panelled room with chandeliers and baby grande piano. I slapped my face. I pinched my midriff.

Just to check my reality, I turned to the Indian channel and there, typically, an older lady with some sort of goitre on her neck was chortling in Hindi while accompanying herself on the harmonium. She was, typically, sitting on a bare platform in front of garish curtains under a photo of Indira Gandhi. And, typically, a blizzard seemed to be howling through the studio.

With a shudder, I quickly switched back to 'Santa Barbara.' After twenty years of short-wave radios and out-of-date Time magazines, all of a sudden I was watching a lovely lady in a slinky, sequinned gown and a handsome if oily bloke wearing a three-piece suit, whispering sweet nothings to each other, in English. I laughed. I cried. I was instantly addicted.

Now, every time I watch a basketball game or Frasier, I remember those early days of western television in India. I imagine Aney's wife wheezing in her room while Aney watches 'Who Wants To Be A Millionaire.' And I think I might like to hook up to the cable here in Wakefield in time for the NBA playoffs.

93. Dances With Wolves, or A Wave Is Still Water. Final Column.

Have you ever had a time when you felt as though wolves were nipping at your heels? I have. There was a headline in 'The Citizen' on Remembrance Day, for example, that read; 'Private Nathan Finally Laid To Rest.' Stuff like that doesn't help. Still, I'm not an overly private person, and the only thing being laid to rest, at least for now, is this column.

Originally, I travelled to India on a hope and a prayer that I might find the meaning of life. What I found was an ancient technique, widely misunderstood in the world, called Dhyan or Meditation. I became fascinated with the idea that a person could actually experience his/her source, the Buddha, Christ or Krishna consciousness. As a Vipassana Buddhist 'bikkhu,' I lived for months on end in silence, meditated, studied scriptures to uncover that truth within myself. And of course the work continued once I met my teacher of over twenty years.

In the winter of '78, about thirty people at the hermitage decided to meditate seven straight days and nights. The decision to do that, however, proved easier than actually doing it. Very few remained by the fourth day. In fact, there were only about nine of us sitting in a semi-circle around Swamiji that night as a fire crackled in its place. We were not allowed to lean against a wall. Nobody could untuck his/her legs. In either case, we were expected to go home, sleep and not return until the end of the retreat.

Be that as it may, nobody said anything about keeping one's eyes closed. And so, as I stared at the fire, watching the ancient scene, I saw people sitting straight, slumping or zooming into torpor. One of the boys was dipping so low as to be nearly touching his head on the ground. Again and again, his heavy head plunged down until he actually smacked it on the carpet. No one else noticed other than me. But, he saw me grinning wickedly, and so he unhappily stood up and stumbled off home.

About an hour later, I noticed a lady leaning back precariously. I could see she was in danger of falling over, which is exactly what happened. She fell right back. However, because her legs were tightly crossed, she actually did a complete backwards somersault. She ended up sitting just as she had been, only a few feet behind. She looked around, embarrassed, saw me watching incredulously, but didn't leave. She moved up again and closed her eyes. Not long after, another fellow toppled over side-ways right onto his neighbour's lap. He got up and left.

Nearly another hour passed as I myself struggled, with eyes open or closed, just to stay awake, let alone repeat my mantra. As I drifted between worlds, all of a sudden I heard an ear-piercing shriek. At once, we all jumped nearly out of our skins, ran outside to see what was happening. But we couldn't find anything going on. After scurrying around the area, several of us stood with Swamiji looking out over the edge of the cliff. Someone insisted a lady must be getting raped somewhere. Someone else said a thief must've been caught in the act. Someone else said it was a wolf.

Now, there are no wolves over there, so we all looked at the fellow who'd said that. By then, we were wide-awake. With some gentle probing the story emerged that he'd let his head rest in his hands while meditating, elbows on the ground in front of him. His arm had fallen asleep, and he dreamt a big, bad wolf was chewing on it. He screamed and everyone had run out of the meditation room. Hearing that explanation, Swamiji just shook his head, announced that he was going to bed, and that was the end of our seven days and nights of straight meditation.

All these years later, I still feel wolves nipping at my heels from time to time. A tree is still a tree. Having said that, however, I should add I've learned that Private Nathan will always be part of this world, a wave will always be water. May God bless us with health, happiness, true knowledge and wisdom.

In India, when we meet and part we often say, "Namaste." That means 'I honour the place in you where the entire universe resides. I honour the place in you of love, of truth, of peace. I honour the place within you where, if you are in that place in you and I am in that place in me, there is only one of us.'

That's the end of the articles but for those of you who are interested in meditation here's a short study on that ancient and highly respected science, and how and why to include it in your life. There'll be no certification at the end of studying these pages. You'll have the same weight, unless of course you eat several copies, and about the same hair and muscle tone that you had before you saw this book. You will, however have a greater understanding of what meditation is, what it isn't and how to do it. And if you really read and understand what I'm writing, you will also enjoy an eradication of some misconceptions surrounding the term and its practice. I should add something about why it may be helpful to seek some form of guidance or a teacher when beginning to examine the science of meditation. One needn't stay for long. One needn't cook or clean for him or her, do anything strange in bed or hand over one's money. What one must do is take advantage of the experience of a fellow traveller who has gone before, who has been up the path and who just might know the tricky twists and turns to watch out for along the way. And there's one more reason to sit with someone whose meditation practice has matured. Those rare people who have dedicated themselves to the process over many years actually emanate a spiritual essence, a vibration that is transmitted to those around them. That may sound terribly mystical, but it's a fact and a quality not to be underestimated.

I'm not a Teacher ...
you're not a Student

On one visit from India many years ago, my dad asked why meditation seemed to have helped me so much, but not my sister, who had also been meditating for many years. She was a devotee of a highly respected teacher, master and guru from India who had been a pioneer in bringing the science of meditation to the western world. Unfortunately, he had passed away long before my sister ever heard of him. I replied that I didn't have a definitive answer to that question, assuming that my dad's presumption was even correct, but I offered a possible explanation. I said that if one wanted to learn to play the piano, it wouldn't really be of any use to sit in front of a photo of one's teacher placed on the music stand above the keys. Why would meditation be any different? Why, for that matter, would religion be any different? It's interesting that all truly enlightened people have said that we are one life, one energy, one love, irrespective of race, creed, color or any other apparent difference. Why does the essential and original message of the enlightened beings through the ages become so perverted as to cause wars? Don't be a Buddhist. Be the Buddha.

That was a piece of advice given to me by Swamiji Shyanji which I have oft repeated and even expanded upon: Don't be a Buddhist. Be the Buddha. Don't be a Christian. Be the Christ. Don't be a Hindu. Be Krishna. Don't be a Sikh. Be Guru Nanak. Don't be a Jew. Be Moses. Don't be a Muslim. Be Mohammed. Don't be a Jerk. Be George W. Bush.

There's really nothing hard to understand about meditation. And yet, it's widely misunderstood here in the western world, and even in its home country, India. From the Sanskrit word, dhyaan, meaning 'For God's sake, leave me alone for a minute', meditation has become synonymous with all things flaky and maladjusted. It's been blamed for wasted talents and even wasted lives. Nothing could be further from the truth. Using myself as a prime example, I admit that I do sometimes forget to put a filter in the coffee machine before pouring in the grains. Who doesn't? Once in a while, I put the Saran Wrap in the refrigerator and the milk in the cupboard. So what? I do all the normal things. Like everyone else, I run, jump and walk while, of course, avoiding the cracks in the sidewalk. And I, along with so many other people who have spent years meditating, have found something so fine, so beautiful and freeing that nothing can compare with it. Rather than blame the proud process of meditation for our foibles, we praise it as the cause of our deep sense of well-being.

My first teacher used to say, "Nathan, stop talking and do your math!" My second teacher used to say, "Nathan, stop daydreaming and do your math!" My third teacher used to say, "Nathan, just do us all a favor and get out." Then I met a teacher who said, "Nathan, the same mind that has gotten you into trouble can get you out of it." In those days I was already a bit out of it and rather hoped drugs might be the answer. But he assured me that was wrong, that drugs would only ruin my nervous system. I developed a pretty nasty tick on the left side of my face after hearing that bit of information. I still prefer Motrin for headaches. But somehow I came to understand that meditation is a powerful tool for training the mind, not to mention getting rid of some uncontrollable twitching. Once trained, I realized, the mind could be used against the enemies of my true happiness, such as a myriad of complexes and even the innate fear of death.

Apparently, the Buddha was known to say that desires are the root cause of all problems. My mother said that lack of money is the root cause of all problems. My friend Danny seemed to think that not having regular sex is the root cause of all problems. Since I tried my mom's solution and Danny's solution for a while, I decided to try the Buddha's, even though I never actually met the fellow. I thought I saw him once at a party, but I couldn't be sure. He was wearing a long, flower print dress, a hat with a feather and six-inch heels. He looked good. Be that as it may, I was pretty concerned about losing my desire for money and women if I began to meditate. Now I see that's not how it works. You don't have to give up anything. You only have to add one thing to your life: a few minutes of meditation daily. Then sit back and watch it enhance whatever else you're into. Watch it help you let go of what you want to let go of. Watch it make you see the cup as half full. Watch it make you happy. One of the most prevalent misconceptions about meditation is that you have to stop your thoughts, kill your mind. What one has to stop, cut or kill is only the concept. Go hunting for small furry animals if you must. But, for heaven's sake leave your mind alone. To allow a wild horse to settle down, it probably isn't a great idea to put it in a very small corral. It's far more preferable to give the creature a large, wide-open field to roam around in. In the same way, it's far better to let the thoughts come and go freely.

Merely sitting or lying down for some time each day and applying the technique ensures a positive result from meditation, in fact. Only your misconceptions concerning what you're doing can get in the way. The very act of stopping for a while will have a positive influence on your day, your life. That's because, actually, you do not meditate. You just need to get out of the way for meditation to happen. It's so easy, yet very few people can do it.

However, this is where the use of a technique comes in. Dhyaan actually means 'attention or contemplation.' Whether a mantra (usually a Sanskrit phrase) or the breath becomes your chosen point of attention, the results of meditation are assured. Done properly and with the right understanding, you will enjoy a quieting of the mind, a heightened sense of well-being and an uncontrollable urge to ride your neighbor's husky around his yard like a rented mule. Done with continuity, you will be well on your way to becoming a contented, well-adjusted person like me, walking happily through life while, of course, avoiding the cracks. There are three states of consciousness that everyone is very familiar with: the waking state, the dreaming state and the deep sleep state. From the moment of conception, the ancient sages have said, a person begins to forget that he or she has a fourth state, which is called Turiya in Sanskrit. This state underlies all the other states, just as water is the essence of the iceberg. So the very act of stopping all your activities and tuning in to the essence of your existence, which is what you're effectively doing in meditation, will take care of a lot. And the benefits are many. In eastern philosophies and scriptures, you'll often read that whatever is transitory cannot be said to be real. You'll read that whatever is eternal is real and true. So this body, mind, ego mechanism is in that case not real or even existing.

The ancient sages said that there is, in fact, no death because there was no birth. The space from whence 'we' come from, to where 'we' go, is considered real. The technique becomes, in the light of the previous paragraph, like an anchor. Utilizing it helps bring one's attention back to one's own self, to the reality of the essential life animating your body and mind. The technique helps us stop. As well, the technique trains the mind to focus like a laser beam, which will have far-reaching effects on your day, your life and, ultimately, your spiritual knowledge. The Vedantic scriptures liken the mind to a monkey flitting from branch to branch, tree to tree. Our mind flits from object to object and from thought to thought. We become so extraverted over the course of the years, or even as each day progresses, that it behoves us to find a way to regroup, so to speak. So, when we've decided to let the thoughts come and go freely while we sit and watch, we merely add one new thought. The phrase, or mantra, becomes a very significant and enjoyable thought as time marches on. All true mantras mean virtually the same thing: "I am the pure life, the essential energy animating all the forms." There is a popular mantra that goes 'Om mani padme hum': 'Behold the jewel within the lotus flower.' There is another that goes 'Amaram Hum Madhuram Hum': 'I am immortal, I am blissful and indivisible.' Another popular mantra goes 'Tat Twam Asi': 'All for me! Me, me, me!' OK, it really means: 'You are the pure life.' All real mantras basically refer to the one life, the one light at the center of all beings, the spark that animates all the forms.

It is often noted that Sanskrit is used for mantras because the vibration of the phrases resonate within the human mind to open certain spiritual channels. For an in-depth dissertation on the vibrational qualities of Sanskrit, I recommend Chaytna's book, 'Let's Learn Hindi' which can be found through her website: www. letslearnhindi. com. I've always used the Sanskrit word, 'Shyam', as my mantra. It's the name of my teacher and a symbol of the power that sustains life. It really doesn't matter what mantra you choose, although Sanskrit mantras are the most recommended. Choosing a mantra and sticking to it is also recommended. Meditation is a technique of being one-pointed, after all. Chogyam Trungpa once wrote that western people tend to try many different techniques, which is like a thirsty person digging many shallow wells but never hitting water. He wrote that we should dig one well deep enough to get to the desired result. Having chosen a mantra, or been given one by a spiritual guide, guru or full-body masseuse, you're ready to begin. My teacher used to say that you should be able to meditate anywhere unless somebody is physically shaking you. On my way to India for the first time, I was compelled to sleep on the rooftop of a hotel in Peshawar after a long and tiring day of travel. The noise level from the crowds up there and the hollering, smoke and smells from the streets below were off the charts. I was convinced meditation would be a wasted endeavor in such a place. But, I had little choice. And after about an hour, in spite of my misgivings, I felt rejuvenated and refreshed. As well, contrary to popular belief, it's not necessary to sit ramrod straight with legs crossed. It's not even necessary to sit at all. You can lie down, settle into a comfortable chair or sit on a cushion with legs out or crossed. Since meditation is first a process of relaxation, let the sense of ease be your guide. You should feel relaxed and comfortable.

It's easy to find a spot where there is very little noise. It's easy to find a spot where there are virtually no pungent odors, unless of course you smell. It's easy to find a spot where you're not touching anything other than the pillows. But how does one get away from one's own mental projections? As I've said before, the first thing to do is not mind your own thoughts. Don't mind your mind. Remember, the same mind that got us into trouble can get us out. The mind is a trickster, a monkey. It will first distract you from your mantra and then make you feel bad for being distracted. Allow your thoughts to come and go freely. Decide beforehand that you won't feel bad about them. Because I promise that you will be distracted again and again. So each time you realize you've been thinking or listening to a noise or feeling pain, pleasure or a strong emotion of some sort, just go back to your mantra without any sense of self-recrimination. There's no need to beat your self up over this. Put the chains back in the drawer. You can even get right into thinking, about your day, your life. You can get into thinking about life itself, pure, free and forever. Just keep returning to your mantra, again and again.

It is important to understand that whatever one perceives and experiences in meditation, just as in ones day-to-day life, is transitory and changing. Whatever one thinks, hears, whatever pain, pleasure or strong emotion one experiences will have a beginning and an end. So, when you meditate it is useful to put your attention on the watcher rather than what is being watched. The same uninvolved observer who was watching as a young boy or girl is the same one who is watching now. As your body has grown and as you've gained more and more skills, qualifications and life experiences, that watcher has never changed. That one has been watching all the changes and is watching still, unchanged, uninvolved. That uninvolved observer has always and. will always be fine throughout the life and even after. Think about that.

Just to confuse the issue, and in spite of what I've said previously about being one pointed, I would offer you another technique that was given to me many years ago. It's called Anapana, with a soft a. It is a technique of concentrating on the breath. I'd also offer you a cup of Indian spice tea if you were here. For now, the mantra and the breath will have to suffice. And, as I've mentioned, it is actually recommended that you choose one technique and stick to it. Anapana is referred to as the maha mantra, the ultimate mantra. The reason is that it's the least tangible, the subtlest point one can attend. There's virtually no form to watch, no form to hold on to with your mind. However, it's a bridge between the part of you that's transitory and the part that's immortal, eternal. Think about that.

The million-dollar question is this: Can you allow the inhalation and exhalation to happen on its own without asserting yourself? Can you stop doing anything and just observe your own breath? While sitting, slouching or lying down, or while waiting to be wheeled in for your bypass operation, put your attention on the nose-nostrils-upper lip area and watch the breath. Don't follow your breath in or out. Watch the inhalation, the exhalation and the space between them. And, again, as often as your attention is deflected into your thoughts, the noises around you or the pain in your chest, that many times you have to go back to your chosen point of attention. And don't bother being bothered by being distracted. Whether you are meditating on a mantra or the breath, you may not think you're having a very peaceful meditation. As I've already pointed out, you may think you're wasting your time. Just keep in mind that rooftop in Peshawar and give peace a chance. There is no such thing as a bad meditation. You may doubt that you can do it. You may doubt that you should do it. I suggest that you be patient and give yourself time. In one of my recent sessions, a lady said that she really didn't understand what she was doing while meditating. That was a valid point. It was a valid point because she was not doing anything. We're not used to stopping. We're not used to letting go. It's much simpler to run around the block for a half hour than to stop all our activities for the same time period. It's the most worthy and yet the most difficult of all activities. And don't get stuck on the technique. You can just watch the space, so to speak. You are the teacher. You are the path. One of the first things you're likely to notice is that the quality of your thoughts will change. You probably won't feel like hollering at your wife or husband so much anymore, tying a tin can to the tail of your neighbor's cat, back-ending the guy who just cut you off. You may even notice some uncharacteristically charitable thoughts creeping into your internal dialogue. If that happens, I would recommend you stop immediately and play a particularly violent video game. You may want to turn on some gangsta rap music and pump up the volume. Of course, if your new thought processes seem strangely soothing, then by all means continue. It won't be long before you'll get the feeling you're looking for.

When one is sitting, continuously placing ones attention on or identifying with the watcher rather than what is being watched, one is essentially developing equanimity. Each time one says 'pain' rather than 'my pain,' or 'pleasure' instead of 'my pleasure,' one is essentially stepping back from the ever-changing phenomenon just a tiny bit. In that way a person will observe again and again how all of ones sensory perceptions, whether pleasant or unpleasant, change. But a person will also observe again and again how the observer, the watcher, seems to remain ever the same. In that way, one is travelling in the right direction and eventually, aside from any deeper effect, an ability to pause before reacting to whatever is going on around you is necessarily developed. And that ability to take a moment, even a split moment, to act creatively rather than react blindly, is incredibly valuable. When a person throws an insult in your direction, for example, and you catch it as though it's a bouquet of roses, the insult loses all its power.

It would be tempting to underestimate both techniques I've suggested you choose between. But before discarding the practice out of hand to return to your Scrabble game, you may find it interesting to dwell on the fact that there are thousands of people around the world who have dedi-

cated their whole lives to doing nothing else. Of course, then you'll have
to figure out if they're all misguided idiots or folks who have actually
discovered a way to answer first-hand those insidious questions that linger
in our minds from early childhood. While everyone is striving for name,
fame and fabulous wealth during this lifetime, people tend to lose sight of
one very important fact. In a hundred years or so, nobody you know now
will be alive. And nobody who is alive will really care who you were.

There are certain things that don't go well with meditation. Smoking
cigarettes, smoking dope and drinking copious amounts of alcohol tend to
be counterproductive. Heroin is just not very helpful. It's a matter of
going from the grosser to the subtler. And in that regard, I would also take
the chance to suggest eating less meat, especially red meat, and consuming
more fruits and vegetables. People who are completely into eating animals
on a regular basis might not appreciate my writing this, but I think it's
really very important that I do. I only hope you don't come after me with
a meat cleaver muttering something about it being all fine if you use the
right spices. If you feel you really must eat some creature's mother or
father, far be it from me to stop you. Lord knows we need our protein. In
fact, nobody need necessarily cut out any pleasures whatsoever. Just add
one more thing to your life. Meditation will help everyone.

And while I'm offending people's sensibilities I may as well mention my
belief in the importance of continence. I'm not referring to the obvious
advantages of curing oneself of adult bed-wetting. After all, there are
effective plastic sheets on the market these days. I've discovered that fact
after extensive investigative research on the subject. Certainly, I'd have to
be insane to suggest cutting down on sexual activity, it being the way we
tend to judge how wonderful we are. So I won't go there at all. This sensitive area of the ancient science of the sages is esoteric and I therefore will
not explain it. It's secret. My lips are sealed. I'm only lightly, gingerly
alluding to the possibility of a certain conservation of energy. I may write
all about it openly in my upcoming book, 'Wendy Does Wakefield.' Until
then, you would of course be welcome to ask me what 'Brahmachari'
means, what the terms 'OJ as,' 'Tejas' and 'Bindu' refer to if you attend my
sessions, although only after several months of dedicated meditation practice. We could eventually discuss it over that cup of Indian spice tea I
promised you. What I can tell you is that, when I returned to Canada in

1998, I was quite amazed to find out how many people had attained miraculous powers rather miraculously. It still seems to me that every second person has the ability to heal merely with a touch. Many don't even need to touch you. They can do it over the phone. There are a plethora of channelers, people able to communicate with angels, crystal bowl healers, psychics, clairvoyants, palm readers, garden variety fortune tellers, intuitives, aura readers, tea leaf readers … It seems that in this new age everybody's sister, mother and brother are powerful healers and teachers. And that's just great. I would only mention that one might be well advised to keep ones attention on the goal. Many years ago Alan Abel, who was with the Globe and Mail in Toronto at the time, came to visit the Shyam Hermitage in Kullu,

India. During his interview with Swami Shyam, Alan asked if Swamiji had any extra normal powers. "Yes, I do," Swamiji said. "I have the power to love everyone unconditionally." I'm quite convinced that greatest of all powers can be only attained by the direct experience of the oneness of all life, the one life permeating all the forms, pure, free and forever.

There's nothing to say one has to meditate or even make enquiries about it. However, if you've gotten this far you might as well read the rest of what I want to say. When one looks up at the night sky and sees all those stars, one has to wonder where it ends. And, for that matter, one has to wonder where it all began. Intelligent people through the ages have continuously wondered where they came from and where they end up after the body dissolves. I haven't a final answer to those questions, not from firsthand experience or knowledge. But, I do know that asking oneself those questions is certainly the beginning of a great journey. And my direct personal experience has left me quite convinced that there is a lot of truth in what the wise ones have always said about our source and our destination. There is more to life than what meets the eye. There's more to me than this body and mind. This is a fact that I know through personal, direct experience.

It has also become extremely obvious to me that, in spite of the many differences, we all breathe the same air, that our hearts all pulsate with the same love of life, and that we all desire freedom. Namaste.

And finally . . .
My Prayer

Dear God, keep everyone safe from problems of the heart
Let lovers not be apart
Save my friends from all forms of pollution
For gastritis, asthma, allergies and helpless dogs, give your solution
Dengue fever's not too cool either
Dear God, keep all free of bubonic or pneumonic plague, leprosy,
Alzheimer's or HIV please
Pigs hearts, mad cows, fleas or lime disease
But for me, dear God, well, dental makes me mental
Save me from the peridontist
Keep me from the orthodontist
If need be I'll not eat, I'll stay in bed, I don't care
Just keep me from the dental chair
For lymph, lung or liver cancer
Hair loss, back pain or cholesterol, give everyone else your answer
Don't let the state of this world turn children into cynics
Dear God, I ask only you keep me from those dental clinics
If this is all too much to ask, of course, or if it's just not fair
Let me see your perfection everywhere.